T0346981

POETRY AND THE LANGUAGE OF OPPRESSION

CARMEN BUGAN

POETRY
AND THE
LANGUAGE OF
OPPRESSION

Essays on Politics and Poetics

OXFORD
UNIVERSITY PRESS

OXFORD
UNIVERSITY PRESS

Great Clarendon Street, Oxford, OX2 6DP,
United Kingdom

Oxford University Press is a department of the University of Oxford.
It furthers the University's objective of excellence in research, scholarship,
and education by publishing worldwide. Oxford is a registered trade mark of
Oxford University Press in the UK and in certain other countries

First Edition published in 2021

Impression: 1

Published in the United States of America by Oxford University Press
198 Madison Avenue, New York, NY 10016, United States of America

British Library Cataloguing in Publication Data

Data available

Library of Congress Control Number: 2021930514

ISBN 978-0-19-886832-3

DOI: 10.1093/oso/9780198868323.001.0001

Printed and bound by
CPI Group (UK) Ltd, Croydon, CR0 4YY

In memory of Jon Stallworthy, with gratitude for his caring intellect, his warmth, and his deeply enriching friendship

PREFACE

My father, his jailer, and I, a fine triangle.
Time on my side, I fling this stone of (rescued?) memory,
Into the river where you cannot step twice.[1]

The task before me concerns the experience and the energies of three words which have shaped the content and the form of my writing, the private and the public aspects of my work, the precision and the imprecision of language. The words are: 'repression', 'oppression', and 'expression'. They meet in an equilateral triangle, with 'expression' at the base, the 'oppression' and 'repression' coming together at the top. The *Oxford English Dictionary* defines 'repression' (*noun*) as derivative of the verb 'repress' which means to 'subdue (someone or something) by force; restrain or prevent (the expression of a feeling); suppress (a thought, feeling, or desire) in oneself so that it becomes or remains unconscious; inhibit the natural development of self-expression (of someone or something)'; 'oppression' (*noun*) as 'prolonged, cruel, or unjust treatment or exercise of control or authority; the state of being subject to such treatment and exercise of authority; mental pressure or distress'; and 'expression' (*noun*) as 1. 'the process of making known one's thoughts or feelings; the look on someone's

---

[1] Carmen Bugan, from '"Butnaru" at the visit with his daughter', in *Releasing the Porcelain Birds: Poems After Surveillance* (Swindon: Shearsman, 2016), p. 23.

face seen as conveying a particular emotion; a word or phrase, especially an idiomatic one, used to convey an idea; the conveying of feeling in a work of art or in the performance of a piece of music'; and 2. 'the production of something especially by pressing or squeezing it out'.

Repression, oppression, and expression are conditions of our existence that involve provocation and response, a constant movement and change which have to do with outer and inner pressure, with a fight between acceptance and resistance, and with having or lacking a sense of agency. By coincidence, these words are morphologically and etymologically related (they all have a sense of pressure) and they are a part of my life, as great forces, in the same way the lines of the triangle touch each other. My own experience of growing up under oppression serves as a starting point from which I can ask specific questions about several aspects of the language of poetry, especially concerning the creative process. Writing from life experience presents one with the task best expressed by Antoine de Saint-Exupéry in his memoir *Wind, Sand, and Stars,* where he faced the struggle of locating the appropriate language that would convey how he survived being blown to sea by a cyclone off the coast of Argentina: 'That is my story. And it is not a story.' The confines of language are very tight: one writes a story (which is commonly understood as a construction of language) about something that is not imagined, but lived through. The story is written from the perspective of being transformed both by the life experience and the experience of working with language, which is slippery and imprecise. Saint-Exupéry explains: 'You cannot convey things to people by piling up adjectives, by stammering.' In narrating the experience for others, something more is needed: '[T]he man who fought tooth and nail against that cyclone had nothing in common with the fortunate man alive the next day.... The physical drama itself cannot touch us until someone points out its spiritual sense.'[2] How one places and resuscitates the actual lived experience (whatever that is) in literary language is, to my mind, every writer's most difficult undertaking.

The question at hand is how to break the triangle that has shaped my own life so that meaningful expression can be fully achieved. Each line has two sides, an internal one (private—dealing with the effects of oppression/repression and writing for the family) and the external side (the public—dealing with published writing, the larger historical context, and literary tradition). No work of literature ever brought injustice to an end even when it stood in direct confrontation to it. But one can extend the base of the triangle (the 'lyric I' in the poem above) until the sides collapse entirely and an awareness of injustice enters literary language without corrupting it. Thus, the experience of oppression becomes part of one's work without suffocating it, part of the freedom one achieves, without impinging on it.

The current undertaking strives to locate specific resources in the lyric language which can be used to press against the language of oppression so that they can help 'to realize a greater good or avoid a greater evil', as Aristotle said in his note on 'The Representation of Evil'.[3] Though the most urgent desire is self-liberation, the most ardent ambition is to find in language the tools with which to counteract injustice. Such desires and ambitions may

---

[2] Antoine de Saint-Exupéry, *Wind, Sand, and Stars*, trans. Lewis Galantière (New York: Harcourt, 1967), pp. 61–2.

[3] Aristotle, *On Poetry and Style*, trans. G.M.A. Grube (Indianapolis: Hackett, 1958), p. 56.

remain elusive but the question must be asked: 'What does one want from language?' As I write this, I am reminded of Czeslaw Milosz's honesty: 'When I wrote in the introduction to *Rescue* that I accepted the salvational goal of poetry, that was exactly what I had in mind, and I still believe that poetry can either save or destroy nations.'[4] I wonder who wouldn't live for a reward such as this, especially when one knows intimately what it feels like to visit a father in chains, to lose a country, to abandon the mother tongue because it has become suffocating? And who wouldn't want to save nations, when the world suffers in so many ways, when one has children for whom she dreams a gentler life?

But what does it take, I wonder, to maintain such a belief in poetry? And if one doesn't wholeheartedly hold a strong belief about language, whatever that belief is, is it worth writing at all? I am guided by Matthew Arnold's definition of poetry as 'a criticism of life' and his sense that the poet is to be judged by the 'powerful and beautiful application of ideas to life—to the question: How to live'. Arnold sees the need for a moral dimension of poetry, which I find indispensable in my own writing:

> the best cure for our delusion is to let our minds rest upon that great and inexhaustible word *life*, until we learn to enter into its meaning. A poetry of revolt against moral ideas is a poetry of revolt against life; a poetry of indifference towards moral ideas is a poetry of indifference towards *life*.

Equally forceful is his observation on the job of the poet: 'You have an object, which is this: to get home, to do your duty to your

⁴ Czeslaw Milosz, *To Begin Where I Am*, ed., Bogdana Carpenter, trans., Madeline G. Levine (New York: Farrar, Straus and Giroux, 2002), pp. 350–1.

family, friends and fellow-countrymen, to attain inward-freedom, serenity, happiness, contentment.'[5]

Poetry and the Language of Oppression will raise more questions than offer answers; and new questions will surface as part of a continuous search into the creative process inspired by the hope that poetry is of real help in providing an illumination of life. Oppression, repression, expression, as well as their tools (prison, surveillance, gestures in language) have been with us in various forms throughout history, so what I am about to say in this book is nothing new. Milosz's belief is lofty, I know, but every step towards the healing resources of language will be a way forward. What I have to say here represents a particular aspect of these conditions of our humanity as they play out in our time, so it provides another instance of the communion, and sometimes confrontation, with the language that makes us human.

C.B., Stony Brook, 9 July 2020

---

[5] Matthew Arnold, 'Wordsworth', in *The Norton Anthology of English Literature*, Sixth Edition, Vol. 2, ed. M.H. Abrams (New York: W. W. Norton, 1193), p. 1413.

ACKNOWLEDGEMENTS

I thank Germina Nagâţ at Consiliul Naţional Pentru Studierea Arhivelor Securităţii (CNSAS) in Bucharest for giving me access to the archive of surveillance documents on my family and for reassuring me that I can publish the entirety of the archive, without the need to redact the names of people in the files. The document cited by CNSAS is OUG24/2008 approved by Law 293/2008 available in 'Monitorul Oficial'. The CNSAS does not provide individuals with written permission to publish family surveillance archives: the rights belong to families who were subjected to surveillance and have obtained the documents. I thank my family for allowing me to publish the excerpts from our archive that appear in the current book in my literal translation. The language of the translations reflects the secret police-speak in the original files: I made no effort to correct the grammar or improve the flow of the transcripts.

I am grateful to the University of Michigan, LSA Honors Department, for the invitation to Ann Arbor as the 2018 Helen DeRoy Professor in Honors, where I delivered a series of public lectures on *Poetry and the Language of Oppression*: I enjoyed a warm welcome from Lisa Broome and Mika LaVaque-Manty and had several very lovely conversations with Donna Wessel Walker over coffee. I thank Carl Schmidt for editing the lectures, and then editing the final draft of the book: he has remained a stalwart reader of my work, giving not only advice but also the love and support which have nourished my writing over many years.

I thank Gerard Lally at the St. Edmund's Hall Writers' Forum at Oxford University for helping me bring the Michigan lectures from their spoken register to the page. Thanks are due to Lucy Newlyn for her wonderful insights on several issues raised in the early versions of these lectures. Many thanks to Christopher Ricks, who has sustained me in so many ways since I have returned to America: I am grateful for the formative conversations about this book as I set out to write it.

I am grateful to Elleke Boehmer at the Oxford Centre for Life-Writing (OCLW), to the Association of Literary Scholars, Critics and Writers (ALCSW), and to The Power of Storytelling (Bucharest, Romania) for inviting me to talk about aspects of writing in the context of politics, oppression, and exile.

I wish to express heartfelt gratitude to Oxford University Press and especially the two anonymous readers who supported this proposal. No book would have been possible without my editor, Jacqueline Norton, who has made the dream of bringing this book to the readers a reality. I am deeply grateful for her enthusiasm and her encouraging words. It was a pleasure to work with Aimee Wright, Patrick Wright, and S. Kabilan during the various stages of the book production.

And finally, my husband and children have provided the cheering on, the 'Is it finished, yet?' daily questioning, and lots of fun to keep me going.

Permissions

Thanks are due to the following publications:

Shearsman Books https://www.shearsman.com/has granted kind permission to reprint poems from my collections as follows: 'Visiting the country of my birth', 'The names of things', 'The house of straw', 'From the beginning', from *The House of Straw* (Swindon: Shearsman, 2014); '"Butnaru" at the visit with his daughter', 'The prisoner's scribe allowance', 'We are museums', 'The house founded on elsewhere', 'A birthday letter', 'A walk with my father on the Iron Curtain', from *Releasing the Porcelain Birds* (Swindon: Shearsman, 2016); 'Rings' and 'Penn Station, NY', from *Lilies from America* (Swindon: Shearsman, 2019).

The following poems from *Crossing the Carpathians* (Manchester: Carcanet/Oxford Poets, 2004): 'The demonstration', 'In the silent country', 'Fertile ground', 'Portrait of a family', and 'The divorce' are reproduced by kind permission of Carcanet Press Ltd. https://www.carcanet.co.uk/cgi-bin/indexer?product=9781903039687

The Romanian version and the translation of the first version of the poem 'The divorce' discussed in the current book was first published in my memoir *Burying the Typewriter: Childhood Under the Eye of the Secret Police* (London: Picador, 2012). Copyright© Carmen Bugan, 2012. Reprinted with the permission of Graywolf Press, Minneapolis, Minnesota, www.graywolfpress.org

Harvard Review Online https://www.harvardreview.org/has granted kind permission to use the text of my reviews of the following books: George Szirtes, *New and Collected Poems* (Hexam: Bloodaxe Books, 2009); Carolyn Forché, *What You Have Heard Is True* (New York: Penguin Press, 2019); Hisham Matar, *The Return* (New York: Radom House, 2016), Rebecca Loncraine, *Skybound* (London: Picador, 2018); and Meena Alexander, *Atmospheric Embroidery* (Evanston, IL: Northwestern University Press, 2018). Amendments to the texts have been made.

An earlier version of my discussion of Wole Soyinka's poetry was first published in June 2015 in *PEN Transmissions* https://pentransmissions.com/(formerly *PEN Atlas*), English

PEN's magazine of international and translated writing as 'Wole Soyinka's poetry: the insistence of liberty'. Grateful thanks to the editors for the kind permission to reprint.

The Manhattan Review https://themanhattanreview.com/reviews-summary published my review of George Szirtes' memoir *The Photographer at Sixteen* (London: Quercus, 2019), a slightly modified version of which appears in this book.

'Lumina Mea' was originally commissioned and printed by MONK magazine, the new platform for exploring consciousness, spirituality and the arts/www.monk.gallery Grateful thanks for the permission to reprint are due to the editors.

Excerpts from George Szirtes' work are printed with kind permission from the author: grateful thanks.

Excerpts from Meena Alexander's poetry are printed with kind permission from David Lelyveld and Northwestern University Press: grateful thanks.

'The Instant' from SELECTED POEMS by Jorge Luis Borges, edited by Alexander Coleman, copyright © 1999 by Maria Kodama. Used by permission of Viking Books, an imprint of Penguin Publishing Group, a division of Penguin Random House LLC. All rights reserved.

Excerpts from Wole Soyinka's poems are printed with kind permission from Methuen: grateful thanks. Finally, special thanks to Andrew Locking for his kind permission to use the stunning cover image. https://www.andrewswalks.co.uk/

CONTENTS

INTRODUCTION

'Visiting the country of my birth'

Visiting the country of my birth

The tyrant and his wife were exhumed
For proper burial; it is twenty years since
They were shot against a wall in Christmas snow.

*

The fish in the Black Sea are dead. Waves roll them
To the beach. Tractors comb the sand. We stand at water's edge
Whispering, glassy-eyed, throats parched from heat.

Stray dogs howl through nights like choirs
Of mutilated angels, circle around us on hill paths,
Outside gas stations, shops, streets, in parking lots.

Farther, into wilderness, we slow down where horse
And foal walk home to the clay hut by themselves,
Cows cross roads in evenings alone, bells clinking.

People sit on wooden benches in front of their houses,
Counting hours until darkness, while
Shadows of mountains caress their heads.

On through hot dust of open plain, to my village:
A toothless man from twenty years ago
Asks for money, says he used to work for us.

*

Poetry and the Language of Oppression: Essays on Politics and Poetics. Carmen Bugan, Oxford University Press (2021). © Carmen Bugan. DOI: 10.1093/oso/9780198868323.003.0001

I am searching for prints of mare's hooves in our yard
Between stable and kitchen window, now gone
With the time my two feet used to fit inside one hoof.

We sit down to eat on the porch when two sparrows
Come flying in circles over the table, low and fast, happily!
'My grandparents' souls', I think aloud, but my cousin says:

'No, the sparrows have nested under eaves, look
Past the grapevine.' Nests big as cupped hands, twigs
And straw. Bird song skids in the air above us.

Into still-remaining rooms no sewing machine,
Or old furniture with sculpted flowers on walnut wood.
No rose bushes climbing window sills, outside.

And here, our water well, a vase of cracked cement. Past
Ghosts of lilac, pear, and quince in the sun-bitten yard, I step
On re-imagined hooves, pull the chain, smell wet rust.

Unblemished sky ripples inside the tin bucket,
Cradled in my arms the way I used to hold
Warm goose eggs close to skin so not to break them:

'The earth will remember you', my grandparents once said.
Here, where such dreams do not come true, I have come
To find hoof-prints as well as signs from sparrows.[1]

To my knowledge, no poet ever changed the course of history, but many dictators did. Poets and dictators, however, have had a long relationship: sometimes they cooperated, especially when poets enjoyed being held in high regard by the powerful; often they clashed, because poets have protested against injustice. Both poets and dictators have an exceptional facility with the language of feelings, valour, and aspirations. They also know that freedom is the soul of humanity and that people are willing to die

---

[1] Carmen Bugan, *The House of Straw* (Swindon: Shearsman, 2014), pp. 72–3.

and kill for ideas held with the strength of convictions. And they know that the battle for the soul begins and ends in language, in particular words, often with the same word that serves the oppressor and the oppressed alike: for example, 'heroism', or 'power', or 'freedom', or 'patriotism'. As the editors of *Tyrants Writing Poetry*, Konstantin Kaminskij and Albrecht Koschorke show, 'Political authority and literary *auctoritas*' enjoyed a 'symbiosis' in antiquity, in which the political sovereign created 'a world from deeds' and the poet created 'a world from words', setting a precedent for more recent times.[2] Indeed, Virgil acknowledges and praises linguistic authority in *The Aeneid*, explaining the power of words to govern people. He gives us an indication of the speaker's character, which informs the public role of poetry:

> As when disorder arises among the people of a great city and the common mob runs riot, wild passion finds weapons for men's hands and torches and rocks start flying; at such a time if people chance to see a man who has some weight among them for his goodness and his services to the state, they fall silent, standing and listening with all their attention while his words command their passions and soothe their hearts.[3]

The tyrant-poets are many, from Nero to Stalin and the contemporary Bosnian Serb war criminal Radovan Karadžić (born 1945) who saw himself as a poet-warrior, re-casting his brutality in lofty language. The tyrant-poets like to see themselves as originators of ideals and as makers and enforcers of social order. They find the eloquent language of poetry conducive to their self-image as

---

[2] Konstantin Kaminskij and Albrecht Koschorke, eds., *Tyrants Writing Poetry: The Art of Language and Violence* (Budapest, Hungary: Central European University Press, 2017), pp. IX–X.

[3] Virgil, *The Aeneid*, Book I: 148–153, revised edition, trans., David West (London: Penguin, 2003), p. 7.

people of elusively untouchable social authority. For their own part, poets, even though they traditionally set themselves in opposition to tyrants, vie for the same language of patriotism, nobility, and liberty, which places their work on the public stage, where it receives scrutiny for its political tendencies and values.

This book is not about poetic freedom in the sense of claiming freedom for poetry, freeing poetry from internal or state censorship, though much will be said about that aspect of the subject. Furthermore, it is not about what becomes of lyrical poetry when it is placed under external or internal political pressure, or about the deep commitment to art for art's sake that has led many poets into exile, though much will be said about this also. And it is not about poet-heroes who endured hardship because they wrote to oppose tyranny. Rather, the following chapters are about the nature of poetry as a form of salvation—from political oppression. By salvation, I mean a sense of recovering aspects of life and freedom which are linked to political persecution embedded in language. What the chapters are intended to convey is a sense of poetry as deeply linked to personal biography, where commitment to the lyric language—the language of feelings, of emotions from the 'deep self',[4] expressed through various poetic devices and figures—is a direct response to the language of political oppression and has become something to be relied upon in order to write oneself into freedom. The aim of this book, therefore, is to talk about politics as a provocation to write oneself free; my concern is not with an attempt to free poetry from oppression, or

---

[4] 'From the depths of the self we rise to a concurrence with that which is not-self.' I will return to this idea of writing that achieves harmony between the inner world and the outer world of language and experience. See Geoffrey Hill, 'Poetry as "Menace" and "Atonement"', in *Collected Critical Writings*, ed., Kenneth Haines (New York: Oxford University Press, 2008), p. 4.

with freeing poetry from political language, or indeed with arguing for one political system as against another. It is in this specific sense of 'writing oneself free' that I want to think about the relationship between poetry and politics.

Poetry, politics, freedom, and oppression will be considered through their manifestations in language that governs our private and public lives. We are born into language and words shape how we understand the world and our place in it. Here I meditate on language in our time, and on how, in the words of George Steiner, we 'can use human speech both to love, to build, to forgive, and also to torture, to hate, to destroy and to annihilate'.[5] Language, in this sense, is itself a manifestation of our human condition. Geoffrey Hill expressed this inherent sense of language as containing both menace and atonement in his essay 'Poetry as "Menace" and "Atonement"'. He wrote, 'It is one thing to talk of literature as a medium through which we convey our awareness, or indeed our conviction, of an inveterate human condition of guilt or anxiety; it is another to be possessed by a sense of language itself as a manifestation of empirical guilt.'[6] Language is imbued with a history of experience, and poetry is not autotelic. In this context, I treat writing as a process by which one achieves freedom and clarity through a hard-won simplicity. As T.S. Eliot said in his poem, 'East Coker V', about writing, one attempts to 'recover what has been lost' and gains mastery over language, 'By strength or submission'. To my mind, the craft of writing, like all other crafts, is a process of invention and discovery, where, in the words of Antoine de

---

[5] D.J.R. Bruckner, 'Talk with George Steiner', *The New York Times*, May 2, 1982, Section 7, p. 13. Accessed online, 5 May 2020. https://www.nytimes.com/1982/05/02/books/talk-with-george-steiner.html.

[6] Hill, 'Poetry as "Menace" and "Atonement"', pp. 8–9.

Saint-Exupéry, 'the perfection of invention touches hands with absence of invention, as if that line which the human eye will follow with effortless delight were a line that had not been invented but simply discovered.'[7]

'Home is where one starts from',[8] says Eliot in the same poem, and there is where I shall start. The considerations of language in these chapters unfold through the story of visiting the country of my birth, the Romania of communist repression of the 1960s through the 1980s, which occasions a revisiting of my sense of personal and poetic identity. I say 'visiting' because I am an exile, and because the return concerns time and language. This visit to my country was first effected by reading the secret police (or Securitate) transcripts of my childhood. The transformation that the reality of the files, and their language, enact on the poetic language is profound. I acknowledge the anxiety in the way I write, to show how the language of the files drowns the voice in the poems, for the truth is that the files draw me out of a carefully built sense of who I have become after leaving Romania and immerse me in their content and non-emotional, yet devastating, language. I write against dictatorship, using the words of the dictator.

---

[7] Antoine de Saint-Exupéry, *Wind, Sand, and Stars*, trans. Lewis Galantière (New York: Harcourt, 1967), p. 42. Antoine de Saint-Exupéry talks about the craft of building an airplane. The more perfect the machine is and the better it functions, he says, the less we are aware of it, shifting our focus to the places in nature it allows us to discover. Thus, he argues, the machine (and in my analogy, the poem, which is a crafted artefact of language) 'does not isolate' us from 'the great problems of nature' but instead 'plunges' us 'more deeply into them' (p. 43). My argument (not new) is that excellence in poetic language rests in its ability to call attention to human nature rather than to itself. It takes a certain humility, not only skill, to achieve this.

[8] T.S. Eliot, 'East Coker V', in *Collected Poems, 1909–1962* (New York: Harcourt Brace, 1963), p. 189.

Writing occupies the uncertain place between the memories I have kept as sacred, as a foundation of my identity, and the memories brought on, or implanted by the records, which re-orient me towards my native country, the people I thought I knew, and my own earlier self. In other words, the new 'place' of writing reflects a fractured identity precariously built with information that sometimes corroborates memories but more often contradicts or supplements them: I have termed this an 'archival identity', which is a public record, after all.[9] My native country and my native language have been transformed into 'places' *before* and *after* the records. The Romania of personal memory is simultaneously a lost paradise and a place of suffering, which I nevertheless left reluctantly. The poems which revisit the Romania of the files are conceived through 'a poetics of quotation marks' that allows me to bring the secret police narrative within the language of poetry: not only to expose it as language of oppression but to reveal it as a narrative that is unerasable, unexcisable, and historical, in that it represents the common memory of my people under totalitarianism.

Implicit in this undertaking is the assumption that these Securitate dossiers are necessary material for poetry, not only because of their testimonial value but as a clear example of complex linguistic constructions used for systematic control of people that bureaucratize the maintenance of fear, dispense with compassion, blunt the soul. These are all part of my past experience, and now part of the voice in many of my poems. Although literature about secret police surveillance in communist Eastern Europe is

---

[9] I first wrote about the files in 'An Archival Identity', published in *PEN Atlas*, 29 August 2013. https://pentransmissions.com/2013/08/29/my-archival-identity-2/.

becoming more widely available in the West with the publication of dissident memoirs, fiction (Cold War spy novels), and memoirs by writers who protested against the communist regimes, to my knowledge no one has transformed state surveillance records into poetry, and, to date, I am not aware of an account of the artistic process as it brings that particular history into the language of literature and makes it part of a critical conversation. The literature of surveillance plays a significant role in understanding how power is wielded in language, and how the individual resistance to oppression is part of our human story.

One aspect of revisiting and rethinking the past is reorienting oneself towards childhood stories so crucial in forming the trust in language on which every writer depends. This reinterpretation was also effected by my reading the files: they have reframed emotionally my early life with its fictions, turning it into something else almost entirely. One of those stories found its way into my father's secret police dossier. What does a children's story have to do with secret police documents evidencing someone's crime against a regime? And what does the story mean twenty-seven years *after* I first copied it from the book, when I marvelled at the noise, the smell, and the neat letter marks of my parents' typewriter? There was a large airy room with a big, heavy oak table in the middle of it. The windows were opened and the grapevine bushes crowded on the windowsill. Perched on a chair was a girl who typed a story about an old woman. No one thought of asking what would become of them both.

I sat at a large table in the Reading Room at Consiliul Naţional Pentru Studierea Arhivelor Securităţii (CNSAS), in Bucharest, in July 2010, with my mother. We were sifting through the stack of penal and informative dossiers kept on my father from 1961 up until our emigration to the USA in 1989. There was the 1983 penal dossier of 'Ion Bugan, condemned for propaganda against the socialist regime'—for typing fliers against the communist government on an illegally-owned typewriter and holding a public protest against Ceaușescu on 10 March 1983. Inside there were photos of the buried typewriter and proofs from the 'scientific analysis' of the keyboard, linking my father to his crime. Among the papers was this fragment from my childhood:

> Once upon a time there was a very old woman who had three sons who were sound of body but weak in their minds. The old woman wanted to keep them close by and devised a plan to convince all of them to build houses in her backyard where they could bring their wives and raise their families. When time came for the oldest son to get married, the old woman was overcome with joy at how she would make her daughter-in-law work all day.[10]

And then the story broke off. My child's hands had got tired of typing coherent things and made rows of letters and numbers for the rest of the page. I must have been between 10 and 11 years old when I typed that. The story found *me*, as much as I found *it* in the improbable mess of time, confiscation, archiving, transfer across the country, from our house to the national secret police archives. I did not remember the story then but I remembered it later, it is a story by the greatly-loved Romanian author Ion Creangă: on re-reading it, I saw that I typed a tiny summary of it in my own words. When I left Romania, I did not know anyone who could not reproduce fragments from his *Memories of Childhood* by heart, and I secretly 'tested' many of the Romanian immigrants for their

---

[10] Ion Creangă, 'Soacra cu trei nurori': I first wrote about this excerpt in a piece called 'About a Story', published on the blog of the American Library in Paris, 11 November 2012 http://alip.quentincunat.fr/about-a-story/.

memories of sensibilities, by mentioning Creangă to them: to date, no one has failed.

As my mother and I collected our bags and headed for the airport, I felt both shaken and touched by the reminder that this story illustrates our instinct as people from the provinces: to share the same house and the same yard for generations, to never leave home. In 2010, when I visited my grandparents' house twenty years after our expulsion, I still found two standing rooms anchored by the new house which the current residents, my cousins, attached to the back walls. That connection between us and our land has become now only a story. The story about the old woman, in the context of the archives, has transformed into a document about a very private and playful moment I experienced as a child. The story itself almost no longer matters: its reframing and re-reading as evidence of the violation of family privacy matter more. Yet I think of the continuity and tradition I expected from life once upon a time. Now that these expectations no longer exist, it is moving to find a trace of them, so there is irony here too: what was taken from me was kept intact. Time stops in the archives, a single moment is preserved on a sheet of paper. It's a museum where one can see what people were reading and dreaming about in the communist Romania of the 1980s.

For whatever it is worth, this biography of my family written by the secret police is a record of hope and dissent that was thought not to exist in my native country at that time. As Dennis Deletant observes in his study, *Ceauşescu and the Securitate: Coercion and Dissent in Romania, 1965–89*, historians, writers, and other intellectuals largely complied because they felt disillusioned, afraid, or were opportunistic, as much as because they had not seen any resistance from the larger population. It is true that very few people had the courage to stand up against Ceaușescu: but it is also true, as Deletant duly notes, that many who did were destroyed quickly and no record has been preserved of their bravery. My parents' fight for justice, solitary as it was, corrects the predominant perception of Romanians as timorous.[11] And now, correcting this perception has become part of revisiting my country as a writer.

In his book, *Language and Silence*, George Steiner has an essay on 'The Writer and Communism', where he characterizes the relationship between politics and literature as one which has led many writers to exile, solitude, and suicide. He writes, 'Communism tyrannizes by exalting man above that sphere of private error, private ambition, and private love which we call freedom.' Steiner argues convincingly that communism 'is a creed penetrated from the very moment of its historical origin by a sense of the values of intellect and art'.[12] This explains communism's exceptional dependence on literature for the purpose of indoctrination and, conversely, the fascination of communist literature with the politics of the time. It also explains how much human beings (whether writers or not) are willing to suffer in order to protect their right to private error, ambition, and love.

This mutual interest between the politician and the writer in a time of totalitarianism creates a linguistic interface, where the language of oppression comes into competition with the language of poetry for a higher ideal, and where the struggle takes place: one language suppresses it, the other seeks to express it. The 'lyric

---

[11] See the chapters 'Compliance' and 'Dissent', in Dennis Deletant, *Ceaușescu and the Securitate: Coercion and Dissent in Romania, 1965–89* (London: Hurst Publishers, 1995), pp. 166–294.

[12] George Steiner, *Language and Silence: Essays on Language, Literature and the Inhuman* (New York: Atheneum, 1972), p. 356.

I' is born in this conflicted area of language where one's private existence unfolds in the context of public duress that is characterized by a language in which the same words are used for exactly the opposite purpose, depending on the context and on who is using them. Seeking freedom in this context requires achieving trust in one's ability to search for truth.

The conflict with communism in my own family in Romania began specifically because my father had expressed his need for private error, ambition, and love, and my mother supported him. Dennis Deletant learned about my father from the appeals made by Amnesty International for his release from prison: 'Ion Bugan, aged about fifty, an electrician from Tecuci, who was sentenced to ten years' imprisonment in 1983 for having driven through the centre of Bucharest with a picture of Ceauşescu bearing the caption "We don't want you, hangman".'[13] The persecution which my parents and we children endured as a result of my father's protest forms the background to my poetry: though the early poems were nothing more than cries of pain, writing them allowed me to 'bring back' my father to the family while he was imprisoned. In this way, I repaired the damage done to our family by those who had power over us. Later, in exile, I wrote my family's story

---

[13] Deletant, *Ceauşescu and the Securitate*, p. 259. Aside from Amnesty International, there were several newspapers (in Germany, Austria, and Spain) and the Index on Censorship, as well as Radio Free Europe, which asked the public to write letters to Ceauşescu, asking for my father's release from prison in the 1980s. Most of those appeals took place around 1986, when my father had already served three years in prison and we at home were under surveillance twenty-four hours per day. For example, see 'Ion Bugan', in *El País*, 5 October 1986, https://elpais.com/diario/1986/10/06/internacional/528937204_850215.html, and 'Romania: Human Rights Violations in the Eighties' from Amnesty International https://www.amnesty.org/download/Documents/EUR390021987ENGLISH.PDF.

as an act of personal healing, to have that 'home in language' to which we could return as immigrants, and to give my children a sense of where they come from. I claimed the right to speak out, even if this required relinquishing my native language and adopting English. More recently, since the Romanian government had granted me access to the family surveillance transcripts and files, I have been writing to rid myself of the narrative of the first nineteen years of my life produced by the secret police, and to expose the mechanism of oppression in language.

Writing myself free has required bringing the political, technical language of the files into direct confrontation with the expressive, intimate, language of poetry. The resulting work is dominated by friction between oppression and freedom in what I have termed the poems' 'language within language', where metaphor searches reality and reality searches metaphor for truth. The poems are founded on the trust that language is wiser than any one individual poet and the process of writing is where hope meets the marvellous. The work I have produced reflects the attendant anxieties and surprises. I have turned to the language of poetry out of a private need, and, in attending to that need, I discovered artistic sustenance and a sense of fulfilment.

But, of course, my encounter with communist repression is not unique. It represents the experience of many Eastern Europeans, whose lives were changed ever since Stalin, Roosevelt, and Churchill met at Yalta in 1945. In a conversation with the vice-president of Yugoslavia, Milovan Djilas, about that historic meeting, Stalin said: 'This war is not as in the past; whoever occupies a territory also imposes on it his own social system. Everyone imposes his own system as far as his army can reach. It cannot be otherwise.'[14] Life behind the Iron Curtain took root, and the Cold War unfolded, bringing with it the terror of nuclear destruction and fear-inducing propaganda. By 1946, my native country, Romania, has removed all the non-communist functionaries from its government. Stalin employed writers as 'engineers of the human soul'. By the time I was born in 1970, Romania had one of the most vicious secret police services behind the Iron Curtain. People were indoctrinated and compelled to live in submission to the Party.

The present book considers poetry's encounter with this larger history too, recognizing, in the words of the Italian poet Salvatore Quasimodo in his Nobel Prize lecture, that the poet is 'concerned with the internal order of man', while the politician is interested in 'the ordering of men'. But the following discussion perhaps also complicates this dichotomy; for I think that communism, at least in the Romania of my childhood, aimed to order society by interfering with people's internal, private lives, and shaping them. In its repression, it certainly shaped people's sense of reality, their trust and ability to see the truth, and their courage to assert themselves. Conversely, the poetry that it provoked is not simply personal; in its expression of the 'internal order' or disorder, it offers a perspective on the consequences of 'the ordering' of people and their language. In its own way, this poetry is a personal testimony of life under oppression. It draws attention to the need for balance, or harmony, between our inner world and the society in which we live. To return to Quasimodo's Nobel Lecture: 'A quest for the internal order of man could, in a given epoch, coincide with the

[14] Milovan Djilas, *Conversations with Stalin*, trans., Michael B. Petrovich (New York: Harcourt, 1962), p. 114.

ordering and construction of a new society.'[15] In other words, the present undertaking aims to consider a larger history as much as being a poet's meditation on writing from personal experience. It also challenges the view that politics and poetry live in separate worlds and therefore in separate regions of language, namely 'governance' and 'aesthetics'.

The war criminal, Radovan Karadžić used poetry in order to convince people to engage in ethnic cleansing and ultimately his poems served to provide an insight into, and evidence, of his guilt. Indeed, Karadžić's case is the first instance where poetry which was 'part and parcel of his war-making activity', figures in a trial of crimes against humanity. In an article that specifically concerns the uses of Karadžić's poetry during his trial, Jay Surdukowski notes:

> While propaganda has long been a fixture of criminal enterprises, only recently have more "creative" arts a step beyond prose – cartoons and poetry – been explicitly subject to judicial scrutiny as was the case at the Karadžić trial. This is an important precedent to ensure complete justice and reckoning with the criminality that has poetry or pretensions to a genocidal poetic destiny at its heart. If a creative art such as poetry has a role in creating the "atmosphere" of "unreason and hatred," it should be part of the reckoning – for reasons of an accurate historical record, as well as for deterrence, and ultimately, vigilance – so that a populace might be on the watch for such art forms being exploited for purposes of war crimes in future.[16]

[15] Salvatore Quasimodo, 'The Poet and the Politician', Nobel Prize Lecture, NobelPrize.org. Nobel Media AB 2020, accessed 4 May 2020., https://www.nobelprize.org/prizes/literature/1959/quasimodo/lecture/.

[16] Jay Surdukowski, 'The Sword and the Shield: The Uses of Poetry at the War Crimes Trial of Radovan Karadžić, the Poet-Warrior', *Law & Literature*, 31(3) (2019): 333–55, (p. 339, and p. 352), DOI: 10.1080/1535685X.2018.1530907.

This is an important development in the treatment of the relationship between criminality and the arts and hopefully it will bring a stronger awareness of the malleability of language, of our uses (and abuses) of it in public discourse, whether in the media, politics, or poetry. Understanding literature as something powerfully *alive*, affecting reader and writer alike, is at the heart of the consideration of poetics in the present book.

People in our time are paying more attention to the reception of language and the words 'freedom', 'oppression', 'public', and 'private' have become more important too. Often they are invoked to represent situations of increased complexity, as our private lives are more often unfolding in the context of social media (a personal choice) and corporate surveillance (not a choice). I think it is important to reassert the value of these words: one person's freedom may be another's deprivation of it, one's freedom of speech, another's terror, while privacy hardly exists at all, as it has either become a form of exhibitionism or it is subject to abuse by technology. The pervasiveness of social media is particularly troubling, especially in relation to news and political discourse, which are dominated by conflicting ideas about what constitutes 'fact-checked' reporting and 'fake news'.

Writers find themselves looking for ways to articulate their sense of our changing world. My aim is to offer a practising poet's perspective on the language of oppression and on searching for a balance between an expressive and a pragmatic poetics, in order to articulate a sense of freedom. How does one write in a world that calls itself free, but perhaps is not as free as it assumes? How does one understand freedom, having been deprived of it, and having understood the costs of claiming it? What exactly is freedom in language? How does literature influence the way we look at conflict? How is language put at the service of life? These are some of the questions raised in this book, which grapples with lyric language both as an expression of the self and as language that considers the reader: the language that aims for Horace's sense of *dulce et utile*. The work of other poets who have responded to their own political realities is discussed in order to offer several perspectives on writing poetry that has arisen from historical upheaval.

The five chapters examine specific aspects of the process of creating literature out of personal testimony, and aim to contribute a poet's understanding of post-Cold War notions of freedom from the perspective of a daughter, a mother, and an immigrant working at what might be called the confluence of languages. The interface between politics and poetry in our time, and the rift between a contemporary poet's sense of private and public identity are explored from the point of view of craft and technique. When politics and tumultuous historical events act not as inspiration, or as obstacles to the creative process, but as a provocation to liberate oneself, the practitioner can come to recognize, with Czeslaw Milosz, that 'I am not seeking an escape from dread but rather proof that dread and reverence can exist within us simultaneously.'[17] The problem of the contemporary poet is thus no longer that of having to choose between art for art's sake and political commitment. Rather, the poet must begin to search for an adequate language to create and celebrate freedom in the deepest sense: the natural, spiritual sense that we are born to enjoy our place on Earth. To use Whitman's

---

[17] Czeslaw Milosz, *To Begin Where I Am: Selected Essays*, eds. Bogdana Carpenter and Madeline G. Levine (New York: Farrar, Straus and Giroux, 2001), p. 387.

words, 'Each of us allow'd the eternal purports of the earth,/ Each of us here as divinely as any is here.'[18]

The process of writing, I argue, is ripe with the potential to *move* (*movere*) poet and reader alike into healing. The discussion stresses continuous reinterpretation and renegotiation of language and freedom, and most importantly establishing a set of values that help us to explore these changes, so necessary in the healing process. What animates these chapters is a conviction best expressed in the words of Pablo Neruda: 'I believe that poetry is an action, ephemeral or solemn, in which there enter as equal partners solitude and solidarity, emotion and action, the nearness to oneself, the nearness to mankind and to the secret manifestations of nature.'[19] I also believe that the books we offer the reader can be a gift. Here are the words of Robert Chandler on Vassily Grossman's novel *Everything Flows*, which he translated: 'if we can speak truthfully and trustingly, our histories can cease to be burdens. Any story, truly told and truly listened to, can become a gift.'[20]

---

[18] Walt Whitman, 'Salut au Monde', in *Leaves of Grass* (New York: New American Library, 1955), p. 135.

[19] Pablo Neruda, 'Towards the Splendid City', Nobel Prize Lecture, NobelPrize.org, Nobel Media AB 2020, accessed 4 May 2020. https://www.nobelprize.org/prizes/literature/1971/neruda/lecture/.

[20] Vasily Grossman, *Everything Flows*, trans., Robert Chandler and Elizabeth Chandler, with Anna Aslanyan (London: Vintage Books, 2011), p. XIII.

1

SOUNDING THE DEEPS OF NATURE

Lyric language and the language of oppression

Jack London's novel, *The Call of the Wild*, from which I have borrowed the title of this chapter, reflects the power of literature to create a complex emotional and intellectual experience. Buck, the protagonist, is a dog grown passive and mild under the good-mannered habits of its master, until it is sold to become a sled dog in the far North, where it endures such terrible abuse, cold, and starvation that it nearly dies. It is at this liminal moment that Buck begins to feel the old call of its wolf nature. In imagining the resilience of the dog, Jack London returns to the 'deeps' of our humanity; he deploys similes that liken Buck's discovery of its inner strength and inner freedom to that of the artist who is completely absorbed in work, and to that of the soldier who is war-mad but refuses to die. London understands language as a resource on which one can draw to convey our deep need for freedom, 'the sheer surging of life'. The following passage has all the movement in the words and all the imagery to both express and somehow induce that thrill of being entirely oneself:

> There is an ecstasy that marks the summit of life, and beyond which life cannot rise. And such is the paradox of living, this ecstasy

Poetry and the Language of Oppression: Essays on Politics and Poetics. Carmen Bugan, Oxford University Press (2021). © Carmen Bugan. DOI: 10.1093/oso/9780198868323.003.0002

comes when one is most alive, and it comes as a complete forgetful-
ness that one is alive. This ecstasy, this forgetfulness of living,
comes to the artist, caught up and out of himself in a sheet of flame;
it comes to the soldier, war-mad on a stricken field and refusing to
quarter; and it came to Buck, leading the pack, sounding the old
wolf-cry, straining after the food that was alive and that fled swiftly
before him through the moonlight. He was sounding the deeps of
his nature, and of the parts of his nature that were deeper than he,
going back into the womb of Time. He was mastered by the sheer
surging of life, the tidal wave of being, the perfect joy of each separ-
ate muscle, joint, and sinew and that it was everything that was not
death, that it was aglow and rampant, expressing itself in move-
ment, flying exultantly under the stars and over the face of dead
matter that did not move.[1]

The Call of the Wild may be read as an allegory of the individual's
reclamation of freedom. Literature, and poetry in particular, can
sound the deeps of nature, and in doing so, provide us with a
sense of stability in an unstable world. Lyric language especially
can interact with the language of oppression in such a way that
one feels what it is like to be oppressed and is also empowered to
imagine a way out.

My work engages with events which took place in the last three
decades of the Cold War in communist Eastern Europe. I write
about repression, dissidence, and exile, underscoring the rela-
tionship between the State and the family. I am interested in the
linguistic mechanism of oppression—how the State acquires and
maintains control over the most intimate aspects of individual
lives through intimidation and fear that are inflicted with lan-
guage. The main question I address here is how one can offer an
account of political oppression in the language of poetry. I explore

[1] Jack London, *The Call of the Wild* (London: Puffin Books, 1982, 2015), p. 46.

the interface between politics and poetry in order to examine how the tension between language that acts to suppress, language that acts to oppress, and language that acts to express can produce literary testimony. Literary testimony is a necessary footnote to history, because it transforms the numbers of those who endure injustice and of those who fight for justice, into people. Literature makes it possible to preserve our individual experiences in our shared memory. In this context, I must state from the start that I am not writing this book in order to condemn communism, since many other political systems have ruled, and still rule people by barbarous means. Rather, the particulars of my own experience serve as examples of injustice and its repercussions, which allow me to reflect on how we use language and how language affects us and our conduct. Such reflection might prove useful when encountering injustice in other contexts.

In my recent poetry I respond to the secret police surveillance archive that the communist government in Romania kept on my family, from my father's first act of dissent in 1960, until our expulsion from the country at the end of 1989, just when the Cold War was coming to an end. The transcripts show how political dogmas can reach into the deepest parts of a person's life. We were one family in millions and our country was one of several in Europe that were dominated by the Soviet Union and an ideology which has transformed the world. Writing from one's own life in the context of a larger history requires a clear understanding of the private and the public perceptions of the self, and how these perceptions balance or upset the lyric voice, and I will explore this issue from several perspectives, as I consider the responsibility for the narrative and the language that I invoke, as well as the sense of identity: personal, national, and artistic. The task of the poetry is not merely to be expressive, but to avoid being politically partisan, so that it reaches into a kinder humanity in its encounter with suffering, as it searches for a way out of it.

Historical Background

The term 'Cold War' was first used by George Orwell in an essay entitled, 'You and the Atomic Bomb', published in the London *Tribune* magazine, on 19 October 1945. Worried about the tensions between Russia and the United States at the end of the Second World War, and about the development of the atomic bomb, Orwell envisioned the future as 'an epoch as horribly stable as the slave empires of antiquity' and 'a peace that is not peace' sustained by world-views, beliefs, and a social structure, rather than by weaponry that could be accessible to the less privileged and used democratically. A cold war, he said, would be a stalemate between two or three powerful nations which would compete over geographical boundaries but would be unconquerable, and would use the nuclear arsenal only as threat or leverage. The battle would be waged mostly with propaganda.[2] The Cold War was fought between the Soviet Union and its allies, on one side, and the US and Great Britain with their allies, on the other. The Soviet Union sealed itself and its Central and Eastern European allies from the western democracies with an ideological, military, and in places, physical barrier that divided Europe: this was called 'The

[2] George Orwell, 'You and the Atomic Bomb', *Tribune*, London, 19 October 1945. https://www.orwellfoundation.com/the-orwell-foundation/orwell/essays-and-other-works/you-and-the-atom-bomb/.

Iron Curtain' by the British Prime Minister Winston Churchill, in a speech he delivered in the USA on 5 March 1946.[3] Tensions intensified by 1947–48 when Russia installed openly communist states in Eastern Europe, and the USA brought Western Europe under its influence.

My native country, Romania, had acquired its Soviet-backed government in 1945. From 1949 until 1962, the government took away people's property and their land against their will in a massive 'collectivization' effort.[4] Earlier on, in 1948–49, it had drawn up a Soviet-style constitution, dissidents were killed, incarcerated, or sent to labour camps, and the communist regime set up the secret police, or the Securitate, which was tasked with eliminating opponents, consolidating power, controlling the public perception of the political realities, and ensuring compliance with the regime. Through specialized training, the Securitate was to become the thought police of the country, a veritable repressive machine, as well as one of the most productive surveillance agencies in that part of the world.

Nicolae Ceauşescu ruled Romania from 1965, replacing the institutional terror practised by his predecessor Gheorghe Gheorghiu-Dej with fear, which was the predominant feature of life up until the 1989 Revolution. When Gheorghe Gheorghiu-Dej died on 19 March 1965, my father, Ion Bugan, was in a prison in Constanţa: he had been caught on 2 March in the Lesovo area of the Iron Curtain in Bulgaria with a friend, trying to escape to

[3] At Westminster College, Fulton, Missouri, 5 March 1946. https://www.nationalarchives.gov.uk/education/resources/cold-war-on-file/iron-curtain-speech/.

[4] See Gail Kligman and Katherine Verdery, *Peasants under Siege: The Collectivization of Romanian Agriculture, 1949–1962* (Princeton, NJ: Princeton University Press, 2011).

Turkey, and was sent back to Romania as a fugitive. Several days later he heard cannon fire outside the prison, and when the jailer came to give him his boiled wheat, he refused, saying he would not eat from the dictator's funeral cake: his contemptuous comment earned him months of solitary confinement when he lived with the weight of 45 kilograms of chains around his wrists and his ankles. My father had been protesting against the communist government in Romania since 1960, and had already spent time in prison for provoking 'social unrest' and trying to escape from the country in 1961 (he was freed in a general amnesty in 1964 but was placed under such stringent surveillance that he had no choice but to flee). As a political prisoner, he was tortured in the labour camps of Braila and the Jilava, Deva, Alba Iulia, and Aiud prisons. In 1969, there was another general amnesty, and he was released from the Aiud prison along with the other political prisoners no one knew about, or no one talked about. By then the Securitate had penetrated every village of Romania and my father was once again under surveillance, enduring the harassment of regular visits to the local police station. The food shortages and the compliance that were endemic in Romania in the early 1980s led him to produce anti-communist pamphlets asking people to stand up for themselves; with my mother he distributed them all over the country. He took to the streets of Bucharest on 10 March 1983.

My father's life in Romania has remained documented in his secret police dossier. In his book, *Ceaușescu and the Securitate: Coercion and Dissent in Romania, 1965–89*, the historian Dennis Deletant writes about my father as one of the fifteen people named by Amnesty International as political dissidents who were incarcerated in the 1980s by a regime which denied the existence of any political prisoners.[5] The other prisoners mentioned by Deletant were my father's comrades; I met some of them many years later in exile in the United States at those reunions of ex-political prisoners and their families that can be utterly strange to the rest of the world. Reading about them in my father's Securitate files makes the horror feel familiar.

According to an article written by the historian Lavinia Stan, and published by the Wilson Center Cold War International History Project, even with millions of records destroyed after the Revolution in 1989, the current secret police archives in Romania total about 35 km of material, every meter containing some 5,000 documents, most of them surveillance files on ordinary citizens.[6] It rivals the East German Stasi archives. The information had been used to monitor, blackmail, discredit, and control the population, so that it would agree to the version of reality portrayed by the government, rather than the actual reality, which was completely different. Yet only a fraction of the documents are accessible to the public. Lavinia Stan says that some of the Securitate surveillance files can be found on the black market, where they can be bought to expose current politicians who had served under the totalitarian regime and now hold positions of power, while others are stored uncatalogued in places to which very few have access.

I was granted access to my family archive, which comprises about 4,500 pages, in 2010 and 2013. Incomplete as it is, it provides

---

[5] Dennis Deletant, *Ceaușescu and the Securitate: Coercion and Dissent in Romania, 1965–89* (London: Hurst Publishers, 1995), p. 259.

[6] Lavinia Stan, 'Inside the Securitate Archives', Cold War International History Project, Wilson Center, 4 March 2005. https://www.wilsoncenter.org/article/inside-the-securitate-archives.

a detailed view not only into the minds and night dreams of each family member, but of the life of our village under siege, and the attempt of the Securitate to isolate us, ensuring that we did not communicate our situation to anyone. It reveals the structure of repression, operated by highly placed military personnel, through secret police officers and agents in a network extending from the capital to the district, the municipality, and the local village, to our relatives and neighbours, and finally my school friends. These documents are both public and intensely private. The historian Timothy Garton Ash, who was under surveillance as a foreigner in East Germany in the 1980s, and who wrote his memoir *The File: A Personal History* upon studying his Stasi file, explained very movingly that:

> What you find here, in the files, is how deeply our conduct is influenced by our circumstances…What you find is less malice than human weakness, a vast anthology of human weakness. And when you talk to those involved, what you find is less deliberate dishonesty than our almost infinite capacity for self-deception.[7]

But what I found in my Securitate file was a teenager under bright observation lights struggling to breathe, and breathing—a girl I almost lost memory of. I found humanity: mine, my family's and my country's, a humanity voicing itself with surprising vigour from under oppression. Good and evil, truth and lie, everything comes alive from those sinister 'observation notes'. Reading these files feels like re-experiencing a violent storm.

[7] Timothy Garton Ash, *The File: A Personal History* (London: Atlantic Books, 2009), p. 223.

My mother was put under surveillance in 1969, when her teaching career had come to an abrupt end because she married a political agitator, who would surely lead her in turn to 'pollute the minds of the young generation'. My sister, my brother, and I were placed under secret police surveillance in 1983, immediately after my father's arrest. The transcripts and documents contain maps and photos of mailboxes in many of the towns in Romania, where my parents put pro-democracy pamphlets, hoping to incite the ordinary people to a revolution; they contain the letters and the pamphlets turned in to the police by scared citizens; and contain the map of my father's demonstration in Bucharest along with the initial interrogation period in the Rahova prison by highly ranked military personnel. Correspondence, telephone conversations, house visits, everything has been transcribed and kept. The surveillance of the family ended in 1989. We arrived in Michigan soon after the Berlin Wall was brought down, and watched the Romanian Revolution on a TV that was given to us. This personal background experience gave me a first-hand knowledge of the power of language—how it can be used as an instrument of oppression and how it can be used as an instrument of resistance. That knowledge has shaped my voice as a writer.

The Language of Oppression

The following passage is a surveillance transcript that explains how my mother, my sister, and I were monitored just before my father was freed. This transcript is an example of what, in the context of the present book, I call 'the language of oppression'.

The surveillance order is dated January 9, 1988, my translation is literal, and I have made no attempt to improve the flow of the language:

Note of analysis

—regarding D.U.I. 'Barbu' opened against named Toncu Mioara previously named Bugan, from the commune of Draganesti, district of Galati.

During the period analysed we obtained information from which results the position and the preoccupations of the objective.

Following the study of the surveillance material we learned that during this period she went together with her three children to the Aiud prison, but she was not allowed to see and speak with her ex-husband. After her return home, the forester Girlescu, a family friend, came looking for her, to ask if her husband has returned from prison as result of the recent amnesty.

It is worth mentioning that during this period old friends and acquaintances ceased to visit the house and as far as Sofica and Stela are concerned, these are neighbours and therefore not in the informing network.

The information from our monitoring devices T.O. and S. reveals that she doesn't maintain connections/friendships with people from other villages/towns, she spends her time knitting clothes which she sells to make money to feed her children.

During the month of November 1987 we received a note from U.M. 0632/5-A by which we were informed that the objective and her daughter Carmen communicate with foreign people.

We mention that we verified these aspects by a combination from which it results that the objective has no intentions to furnish information about her husband to foreign persons.

We report that the objective is a member of the party, who works at the knitting factory 'Earnest' in Tecuci.

In view of these aspects that result from monitoring her, we propose to further resolve the following questions:

—If she engages in hostile activity against the political system of our country

—The forms and methods that she uses in this hostile activity

—Understanding her relationships and their nuances, especially those from other localities

—Understanding if she tries to get in touch with foreign radio stations

—Documenting the activities that she engages in according to the warning and instructions she received –00190/1987

In order to verify the above, we take the following measures:

1. Seeing how the informer 'Calin' often goes to help her with yard work, he will be re-trained to find out the following:

—if the objective listens to news transmitted by foreign radio stations and if she comments on these with friends and with her two daughters, respectively Carmen, student in the XII-th year at the Agro Industrial high school of Tecuci, and Loredana, student at the professional tailoring school in Focsani.

> TERM—30.03.1988
> EXECUTES—Major. Baciu Ion
> IN CHARGE—Colonel Huhulea Mihaita

—identifying all the persons who visit her at home, after which they will be checked against the Securitate records held by us

> TERM—30.06.1988
> EXECUTES—Major. Baciu Ion
> IN CHARGE—Colonel Huhulea Mihaita

2. The informer 'Mircea Alexe' will be re-trained with duties to establish the following:

—if during her commute from home to Tecuci the objective comes in contact with anyone outside the village/unknown in the village

> TERM—30.05.1988
> EXECUTES—Major. Baciu Ion
> IN CHARGE—Colonel Huhulea Mihaita

—in order to double-check the materials produced by this informer, he will be guided to go periodically at the house of the objective where the informer 'Calin' will be asked to make his visits at the same time.

3. Each of these two informers will be instructed about what to say in order to approach the subject about the situation of her husband, as well as other issues of informative interest to us. During this time, the group T.O. will be instructed to record the entire conversations.

>TERM—30.06.1988
>EXECUTES—Major. Baciu Ion
>IN CHARGE—Colonel Huhulea Mihaita

4. Taking in study a person in order to recruit at the workplace, respectively the knitting section, in order to establish the following:

—what kind of comments she makes about her ex-husband

—if she comments about what she hears at foreign radio stations

—what are her intentions once her ex-husband returns home

>TERM—30.03.1988
>EXECUTES—Lieutenant Colonel Magdalinoiu
>Gh. and Major. Baciu Ion
>IN CHARGE—Colonel Huhulea Mihaita

5. We will demand, from the contra-information officer at the Aiud prison, information about the objective during the period when she will go to visit her ex-husband, and information about everyone she comes in contact with during the same period.

>TERM—30.06.1988
>EXECUTES—Major. Baciu Ion
>IN CHARGE—Colonel Huhulea Mihaita

6. Linking for the purpose of monitoring the daughter of the objective, Carmen Bugan, student at the Agro-industrial high school in Tecuci with the source 'Cornelia' from the network of Comrade Lieutenant Colonel Mitrut Ion to establish if she makes comments regarding the act of her father, as well as other aspects that interest our organs.

>TERM—30.01.1988
>EXECUTES—Lieutenant Colonel Mitrut Ion
>IN CHARGE—Colonel Huhulea Mihaita

7. The same information will be demanded from the I.J Vrancea about the daughter Loredana, student at the professional tailoring school in Focsani.

TERM—25.02.1988
EXECUTES—Major Baciu Ion
IN CHARGE—Colonel Huhulea Mihaita

8. We will continue the measures of monitoring with the source 'S', concomitantly with reporting at U.M.0647 Bucuresti to keep her under scrutiny in order to detect if she sends anything outside the country

TERM—25.02.1988
EXECUTES—Major Baciu Ion
IN CHARGE—Colonel Huhulea Mihaita

Depending on the monitoring situation we will also take other measures.

CHIEF OF THE MUNICIPAL SECURITATE   PRINCIPAL
                                      MONITORING
                                      OFFICER
COLONEL   MAJOR
HUHULEA MIHAITA   BACIU ION
AGREED TO BY
CHIEF OF DISTRICT SECURITATE
LIEUTENANT COLONEL
DUMITRU VASILE
BI/GP
RD/00233/38/1 EX.
9.01.1988

Even through the fog of memory I still remember how I tried to avoid talking about my father and how suspicious we were of everyone. Yet, at the same time, I blamed myself for not trusting people, thinking that I was paranoid. Those were the years when the secret police had keys to our house, came and went as they liked, and bragged to neighbours about hearing the sobs of my little brother. They spread rumours around the village that my father had killed himself in prison; they instructed people to attack and discredit us in public. Those who were truly scared did not even look at us; those with a mission asked direct questions. And then there were those whose behaviour we simply did not know how to interpret. Decades have passed since and this provides evidence at least that I was in my right mind when I cut conversations short and interpreted any sign of friendship and care as suspicious. If there is a legacy of this total surveillance on my family, it is the distrust of people we have carried with us in our later life. I was right not to trust, and that is how I protected myself.

'Friends and acquaintances ceased to visit the house': how well said! In our isolation we learned to trust and support each other. This was not as good as being part of the world, but that had to do for those prison years. Our closeness from that time carried us through periods when we could have lost each other. There was no way we could have talked to anyone foreign, or that I would have talked to Radio Free Europe. The Securitate invented the whole report from some military base, and used it as a reason to keep themselves employed.

The Instinctual: The Interface Between the Language of Oppression and the Language of Poetry

I start from the condition of oppression articulated by the transcript of the surveillance. I realize that this is an extreme definition, an extreme example of what I call 'the language of oppression' but it is language which was prevalent during the Cold War, and it shares features with the language used to oppress in other environments. The language by which we were silenced is technical, cold, exacting, bureaucratic, and intimidating. Informers were equipped with listening devices catching every word, and provided with instructions and microphones to double-record conversations, so that these people could be tested, in their turn, for their industrious work. This was an apparatus of betrayal that made victims of everyone: the oppressed and the technicians of the oppression. Though I have seen the transcripts decades after the actual surveillance, we, as a family have felt the brunt of surveillance as it was happening: interrogations, isolation, and intimidation.

In my journey as a poet, I set out to traverse these territories of language and arrived at the thrill of several lines of poetry written by the American Walt Whitman, whose work I encountered as a fresh immigrant in Michigan after Ceaușescu and his wife were executed, and the political landscape began to change. Whitman's 'Salut au Monde' is a remarkable poem, which gave me strength in my early twenties, as I was beginning to define a poetics, and a poetic technique that would help me draw on my life story: 'Each of us inevitable,/ Each of us limitless—each of us with his or her right upon the earth.'[8]

On the face of it, the language of oppression takes away that which the language of poetry is not truly able to restore in any direct or straightforward way. In the Secret Police-speak of the file quoted above our suffering is a matter of bureaucracy, and my feelings for my father were the subject of a work order that was signed by several people. Yet, it was particularly at the time when

---

[8] Walt Whitman, 'Salut au Monde', in *Leaves of Grass* (New York: New American Library, 1955), p. 134.

those orders were drafted that I was writing poetry in which I was expressing a loss, filling the absence with an imagined presence of my father drawn from memory. I gave the poems to my mother and my sister to read quietly, so that the secret of our feelings was not recorded by the microphones we knew were placed around our house: thus our desire for happiness and stability was preserved. Poetry—its rhythmical, incantational language—brought consolation into our lives, working its song against the grain of the language of helplessness. It was a fluent reminder that despite the handicapping language of betrayal, we were whole people who were still capable of feeling. It was at that early moment in my writing that the triangle between oppression (by the State), suppression (by fear), and expression (from a need to survive) was formed: those early poems represent the self, pushing against the two forces on either side, even as it was being defined by them.

These extreme situations call to mind the narratives one constructs in order to survive. Coming to Whitman, years later, in English, with the experience of having feared for my family's life in the prison of our own home, shaped my understanding, and appreciation, of his poem, changing thus both the reader and the writer I would become. I set out to write a poetry in which I declared my inner freedom. Yet poetry does not restore freedom where the language of oppression obliterates it: it cannot be used to overwrite injustice, declare an end to wars, bring someone back from prison, or do away with tyrants. Nevertheless, to borrow an expression from Jack London's *The Call of the Wild*, it can 'sound the deeps of nature', because it is language that nourishes our imaginative faculty to the point where we can vicariously experience being fully alert and alive, experience that 'surging of life'. At its best, poetry is able to tap that indispensable freedom which

Jean-Jacques Rousseau equates in his book *The Social Contract*, with humanity: 'To renounce freedom is to renounce one's humanity.'[9]

In his 'Preface to *Lyrical Ballads*', William Wordsworth has said that poetry is 'the spontaneous overflow of powerful feelings: it takes its origin from emotion recollected in tranquillity'.[10] Such an 'overflow', tempered by the reason required by the creative process, in order to produce work that matters, rather than work that merely shocks, is the exact opposite of the language of fear that had taught me to avoid expression at all costs. The tension between the suppression of the self and the need to break free from oppression can be used productively in the language of poetry. Oppression and freedom wage their battle as powerful feelings in the language of poetry: they meet on the ground of our instinct for self-preservation. Poetry puts melodious words where silence has been imposed or self-imposed: it gives voice to the self in its pain and its reach beyond pain. It gives shape to language so that it does not come out as a howl. It works against the censor with speech that has been considered and weighed. It can cleanse language.

Bertolt Brecht wrote a beautiful short poem in which he said that in the hard times 'Yes, there will be singing./ About the hard times', implying that suffering doesn't silence song, but changes it.[11] 'Lyricism', says the *New Princeton Encyclopedia of Poetry and*

---

[9] Jean-Jacques Rousseau, *The Social Contract*, trans., Maurice Cranston (London: Penguin Books, 1968), p. 8. I will discuss Rousseau's categories of freedom—natural, civil, moral—in Chapter 2.

[10] William Wordsworth, 'Preface to *Lyrical Ballads*', in *The Norton Anthology of English Literature*, 6th edition, ed., M.H. Abrams (New York: W.W.W. Norton, 1993), p. 151.

[11] Bertolt Brecht, 'Motto', in *Against Forgetting*, ed., Carolyn Forché (New York: W.W. Norton, 1993), p. 27.

Poetics, is the quality of poetry that is expressive, musical, rich in feelings, something Hegel might have identified as an 'intensely subjective and personal expression' without its necessarily conforming to the requirements that it is sung or composed according to an exact form that can strictly be described as musical, though the essence of the lyric remains in the repetition of sound that carries forth the meaning in such a way that we can recognize the musical origins of the genre.[12] Hegel's definition of the lyric as an 'intensely subjective and personal expression' is what interests me here, for it fulfils the self; it provides the right language which can celebrate the one, unique, irreplaceable, inevitable essence of the individual that Whitman also talks about: a self which cannot be blurred into masses and historical currents, but one which thrills in the being like Jack London's Buck. But being intensely subjective and personal does not mean being removed from the suffering of others, for one writes for others: it is important to remember here Shelley's concept of 'sympathetic imagination' by which he encourages the poet to 'make the pains and pleasures' of others one's own, to put oneself 'in the place of another and of many others' and to see 'Love' as the greatest moral force there is.[13] Thus, poetry is the threshold that writer and reader cross from silence into speech, where one retains the self but also cares for others.

There are other qualities of lyric poetry which have become useful in my own writing over the years, especially as it took on the

[12] James William Johnson, 'Lyric', in *The New Princeton Encyclopedia of Poetry and Poetics*, ed., Alex Preminger and T.V.F. Brogan (Princeton, NJ: Princeton University Press, 1993), pp. 713–27; 714.

[13] Percy Bysshe Shelley, 'A Defence of Poetry', in *The Norton Anthology of English Literature*, 6th edition, ed., M.H. Abrams (New York: W.W.W. Norton, 1993), p. 759.

language of oppression. One of them is Lascelles Abercrombie's idea of composing a language in which music is intrinsic to delivering the meaning together with the image, the thought, and the emotion. He says, 'A poet does not compose *in order to* make of lang. delightful and exciting music; he composes a delightful and exciting music in lang. *in order to* make what he has to say peculiarly efficacious in our minds.'[14] It is in this sense that I think of poetic sensibility, and music in my case does not mean form or meter but a fusion of words that have travelled through several languages, where sound and meaning carry that past in order to convey feelings and ideas. Like epic poetry (which is narrative) and dramatic poetry, lyric poetry has been with us for millennia, its history following our experience. Its formal versatility—from love songs to hymns and prayers and meditations on life and death—and its ability to adapt both to the objective reality and the subjective (autobiographical), the political and the elegiac, ensures that to our day 'it has become one of the chief literary instruments which focus and evaluate the human condition'.[15]

The language of oppression has been present ever since human hierarchies were invented and slavery began: it has adapted and gained sophistication with time and with the various kinds of oppression people have inflicted on one another. I suspect the use of euphemisms is the chief characteristic of a language designed to oppress: how easy it is for murderers to say 'ethnic cleansing' or 'Final Solution' to cover up stomach-churning brutality! How convenient it is for a rapist to say that a woman 'plays hard to get'! And how noble it is for a tyrant to say that a dissenter is a

---

[14] Johnson, 'Lyric', p. 715.
[15] Ibid., p. 726.

'criminal', an 'unpatriotic' person, and 'an enemy to our way of life'! The word 'democracy' is invoked by all political systems, no matter how dictatorial. This language, by dislodging the meaning of words and introducing obscurity in order to obfuscate and hide the intentions of the user, or simply numb the mind of the populace, attacks the individual's primordial trust in life, creating a narrative of powerlessness, of futility: it is a highly skilled language meant to reduce the individual to a being without will; it meets us at the deepest emotional and intellectual level where we can be destroyed. Bringing the expressive lyric language into contact with the suppressive language of oppression takes poetic utterance to the deeps of our nature.

Here is an example of a poem I wrote in order to portray a situation *in extremis*, in which I tried to call attention to the individual against mass suffering. It is about the experience of solitary confinement. On several occasions, my father spent several months at a time in prison cells deep underground, where there was no daylight. I have asked him what kept him alive and what kept him sane. He explained that it was important to tell himself that he was not going to let the torturers win over him, over his mind and spirit. He spoke about giving lessons on how a transistor is made, using the soles of his boots as a blackboard. Prisoners used soap, matches discarded by guards in the courtyard, saliva, and dust from the walls of their cells, and they wrote things on bars of soap, on the walls: stories, drawings, maps, poems. The prisons were often thought of as 'second universities'. I asked him about poems in prisons and he said the poets were writing on soap, on boots, like everyone else. I thought about those poems 'walking' in the cells, in the courtyards, and imagined traces of destroyed, disfigured words as they were stomped in the dirt. I thought about how poetry, like a ray of inner light, is born in the darkest places where literally, and figuratively, light is blocked out. And if poetry is traceable in such places, then it is capable of bringing more of us together against oppression, by showing the suffering in plain light so that we can all see it for the affront to life it represents.

Decades later, my father and I went inside 'his prisons' and there I saw writing on the walls. In the most solitary and desperate moments of their lives, in the liminal states where they had to consider how their courage to speak truth to power had landed them in what were called 'extermination rooms' (rooms where prisoners were held, waiting to be called to be shot), people reached into language, for words, and they wrote prayers on the walls of their cells. This is what kept them human. The poem 'The prisoner-scribe's allowance'[16] in which I tried to convey my sense of the humanizing power of language, was prompted by the writing I saw in the underground cells in the Jilava prison:

The prisoner-scribe's allowance

Walls are manuscripts and finished books, illuminated
With what the poet found in his cell: words of prayer
Snagged around the throats of rats, weaving the soul

With the spider's net, working its way in the darkness,
By the boarded window that only serves to remind him
Of the sky and air he could not allow himself to dream for.

Beware the dreams inside those rooms, they spring at you
For a clean kill: 'Punishment must be like this', my father said,
'after all, you tried to change a country; don't dream in there.'

[16] Carmen Bugan, 'The Prisoner-scribe's allowance', in *Releasing the Porcelain Birds* (Swindon: Shearsman, 2016), p. 37.

The guards do not give the prisoner-scribe a pen: that would
Turn the scribe into a man. He is left alone with the walls.
But what riches those walls, the souls of others spilled

Out on their cement face, their ghosts dancing in the shadows
Of the scribe's mind, material for books, four canvases wide open!
And forty-five kilograms of chains to turn into writing instruments:

The rust, the dried blood, here's the ink. He chooses the wall
By the invisible window and begins to write with the links of the chains
Moving his body around, etching the letters into the cement,

Until the first line comes out: 'Our Father who art in Heaven!'
He looks at his work, he has written over someone else's line—
He writes between another's lines 'Hallowed be Thy Name'

And beside another's, 'Thy Kingdom Come':
Then he illuminates the manuscript, now his nail is the pen
Ink the blood on his knuckle, he is instrument.

October 2013–January 2014

Freedom is taking oneself out of powerlessness and inhumanity. The prisoners who perished had written prayers on the walls with their chains and with the blood from their knuckles. Before their torturers destroyed their bodies, they had freed their own souls— they had written out whatever was in their minds. To me, this is evidence that freedom is a prerequisite of life itself. As a poet who was privileged to go and see such places, I must give a voice to the past.

A poet who was also a prisoner, and whose writing pursues liberty, is Wole Soyinka. Here I would like to take a brief look at his work, because it offers a robust faith in language despite adversity, a faith, I must add, many of us lose when we look at the abuses taking place in our time, such as racism, discrimination, the shocking differences between the lives of the poor and those of the rich.

Wole Soyinka's Poetry: The Insistence on Liberty

The Nigerian Nobel Laureate Wole Soyinka's poetry is part of an extraordinary opus including drama, novels, memoirs, and criticism.[17] Soyinka writes in English and he brings to the language rich flavours of African names, folklore, and landscape, in a register that marries his country's heritage with European tradition. Like his other writing, his urgent poems draw deeply on the mythology of the Yoruba tribe and the local culture, yet they reverberate with what he calls his 'abiding religion – human liberty'.[18]

Soyinka's poetry crosses the Mediterranean like a boat filled with African people risking their lives, whether in search of freedom or a better economic life. 'No one knows my name', laments the speaker of his poem 'Migrations', which has been etched on the graves of refugees who did not reach the shore of Italy alive.[19] Soyinka's poem, called by the Italian authorities a *carezza* (a caress, soothing touch) performs a gesture akin to keening for those who died, bringing comfort to their families. It bridges the deadly gap between a continent that sheds its people into the sea and a continent that looks bewildered at the human loss. It rests at the uncomfortable boundaries between those who have and those who have not, remaining engaged with the real world.

---

[17] An earlier version of 'Wole Soyinka's poetry: the insistence of liberty' was first published in *PEN Transmissions* on 4 June 2015; https://pentransmissions. com/2015/06/04/wole-soyinkas-poetry-the-insistence-on-liberty/.

[18] James Gibbs, 'Profile of Wole Soyinka', *Index on Censorship*, 13(3), 1984, 50–42, DOI: 10.1080/03064228408533738.

[19] Wole Soyinka, 'Migrations', cited in Sine Plambech, 'Researching Migrant Arrivals, Births and Burials Across the Mediterranean', Ammodi, 6 December 2017, accessed on 21 May 2020; https://ammodi.com/2017/12/06/researching-migrant-arrivals-births-and-burials-across-the-mediterranean/.

Born in 1934 and educated in Nigeria, Soyinka gained a doctorate from the University of Leeds in 1973 and worked at the Royal Court Theatre in London. In 1960, he returned to Africa. His writing opposes colonialism and political corruption, and reflects a commitment to the dignity of people. In 1967, during the Civil War in Nigeria, Soyinka wrote an article in which he appealed for a ceasefire. For this, he was imprisoned and sent to solitary confinement for nearly two years. His experience as prisoner led to work imbued with a personal sense of sacrifice—a personal testimony—for the way in which poetry fights for justice.

His collection of poems *A Shuttle in the Crypt*, which he describes as 'a map of the course trodden by the mind, not a record of the actual struggle against a vegetable existence',[20] intimates the agonies of solitary confinement. His poems are by turn meditative, prophetic, and angry. Yet they pursue a sense of resilience. In the poem, 'To the Madmen over the Wall', the speaker refuses the descent into madness even as he shows to the reader the extent to which the mind is wrung by incarceration: he hears the others howl, he knows they are all 'companions' floating on the 'broken buoy' and yet, he says, 'I may not seek/ The harbour of your drifting shore.'[21] The poem 'When Seasons Change' meditates, in high register, on the solitude of confinement; death hisses in this poem: 'Shrouds of seasons gone, peeled/ From time's corpses, mouse-eaten thoughts' have become 'shrapnels from the shell of vision' and 'Cobweb hangings on the throne of death.'[22] Wilfred

---

[20] Wole Soyinka, 'Preface', in *Selected Poems: Idanre, A Shuttle in the Crypt, Mandela's Earth* (London: Methuen, 1989), p. 95.

[21] Wole Soyinka, 'To the Madmen over the Wall', in *Selected Poems*: p. 115.

[22] Wole Soyinka, 'When Seasons Change', in *Selected Poems*: p. 114.

Owen's war poems, Yeats, Eliot, and Shakespeare come to mind when reading these lines, which make that great visionary gesture even as they intimate the paralyzing presence of death. In a world where engaged poetry either sounds like propaganda or is ignored as such, there is a lot to learn from Soyinka's defiant language and his ability to face the hardest truths as a poet.

Since 1986, when Wole Soyinka received the Nobel Prize for Literature for works in which he 'fashions the drama of existence' with 'poetic overtones', he has been sought as a speaker and lecturer all over the world while continuing to hold teaching posts in Nigeria. He brings with him the feeling of the wider human community and a sense of conviction about art's necessity when dealing with difficult subjects.

When I first encountered Soyinka's work in the late 1990s, it was these lines that kept going through my mind: 'Slaves do not possess their kind. Nor do / The truly free' ('Funeral Sermon, Soweto').[23] Slaves do not possess because they know what it is to be owned by another: they want nothing to do with that pain. The free understand the respect for boundaries. But the devastating reality has to do with the precise sense of possession—each understand their kind—and we know that as long as we do not see others as our equals, we dehumanize and we (dis)possess. The history of slavery is long. Freedom also means keeping an even keel in times of chaos, even as one recognizes that suffering breaks the mind, unhinges us. Soyinka writes about the discomfiting reality of our 'civilised world' with clarity and depth. His poems think actively, they are *pensiero poetante*. What makes me return to

---

[23] Wole Soyinka, 'Funeral Sermon, Soweto', in *Selected Poems*, p. 210.

Soyinka's poems is his insistence on resilience and liberty, and the way in which he works this insistence into a language that remains in the heart and mind long after the book is closed. Literature and poetry in particular do not necessarily transform pain as much as they give it voice in order to transform *us* into people who can *sense* another's person's suffering. There is place and space, and scope in literature to create inside each of us, poets and readers alike, that sympathy for our fellow human beings. We read poems such as Soyinka's and, because of them, we cannot look the other way. We must appreciate that great poetry can be born from nightmares and it is born precisely to fight against those nightmares.

The Public Role of the Poet and the Public Recognition of the Power of Poetry

The power of lyric language, for good or ill, has long been recognized, and during the Stalinist repression poets and writers were enlisted in brainwashing the masses by providing language which would compel them to obey authority. The literary current predominant in 1930s' Russia was known as 'socialist realism': a literature that was to instil in the population a passion for socialism. The project was based on manipulation described by Stalin in terms of engineering. The doctrine was born in the house of Maxim Gorky on 26 October 1932, ahead of the First Congress of the Writers' Union, when Stalin exhorted writers to create in words the vision he would create in deeds: 'The production of souls is more important than the production of tanks.... And therefore I raise my glass to you, writers, the engineers of the human soul.'[24] The socialist realist doctrine had lasted into my lifetime in Romania, and produced many obedient souls. Those writers who did not sing the Party tune were shamed, humiliated, censored, exiled, or killed. There existed a blend of political and literary language during that period that serves as a reminder about the language of power and how power is maintained through language.

George Orwell remarked that 'political language is designed to make lies sound truthful and murder respectable, and to give an appearance of solidity to pure wind' ('Politics and the English Language').[25] Many murders have been committed since Orwell wrote these lines, and so many of them have been made to sound respectable. The power of political language lies in its ability to remain vague, while it hints at narratives that often give people a false sense of security.

Political oppression could not exist if people did not participate in it to some extent. Aside from the brute force of the dictator and his tyrannical regime which come in clichéd images of death as punishment for whoever speaks against them, there is the far more dangerous intellectual trap into which people fall as they seek a sense of stability in their society. The 'vulnerability of the twentieth century mind to seduction by socio-political doctrines'[26] has been discussed by Czeslaw Milosz in his book

---

[24] Joseph Stalin, speech at the house of Maxim Gorky, 26 October 1932. See also, Hilary Chung, ed., *In the Party Spirit: Socialist Realism and Literary Practice in the Soviet Union, East Germany and China* (Amsterdam: Rodopi, 1996), pp. 3–4.

[25] George Orwell, 'Politics and the English Language', in *George Orwell: Essays* (London: Penguin, 1994), p. 359.

[26] Czeslaw Milosz, 'Author's Note', in *The Captive Mind*, trans. Jane Zielonko (London: Penguin, 2001).

The Captive Mind, where he shows how the tyrannical regimes in Europe had the power to enslave people with ideas, and how his own cry for intellectual freedom led him to what he called 'the worst of all misfortunes', exile.[27] Explaining his own choice as a poet who was directly confronted with the Leninist-Stalinist doctrine in Poland in 1945, he acknowledged that, if he had chosen to join the intellectual orchestra of oppression, he 'the poet' would have had his place all marked out for him with 'the first violins'. He described the socialist realism of Stalin as a system that 'preaches a proper attitude of doubt in regard to a merely formal system of ethics but itself makes all judgment of values dependent upon the interest of the dictatorship'.[28]

But it is Milosz's explanation of his personal resistance to tyranny which interests me here. The resistance for him happened at an emotional, instinctual level, which I think is absolutely crucial in bringing oppression and freedom onto the deeper ground of our feelings. He writes: 'My own decision proceeded, not from the functioning of the reasoning mind, but from a revolt in the stomach.... the growing influence of the doctrine on my way of thinking came up against the resistance of my own nature.'[29] Milosz's resistance is essentially the nerve of life. He returns to the instinct of freedom that we also find in Buck: the subjective, individual ground that poetry taps as a source. It forms the basis for his equally powerful conviction that the job of the writer is also 'to keep ward and watch in the interests of the society as a whole',[30] a conviction which returns to a principle held by Aristotle. Of poetry and the representation of evil, Aristotle said:

[27] Czeslaw Milosz, "Preface", *The Captive Mind*, p. XIII.   [28] Ibid., p. XIV.
[29] Ibid., p. XV.   [30] Ibid., p. XIV.

As to whether anything which is said or done is right or not, one should not consider only whether that particular statement or action is good or bad, but the character of the person speaking or acting, the other person affected or addressed, the time, the means, and the purpose, as, for example, to realize a greater good or avoid a greater evil.[31]

Setting in motion and maintaining the mechanism of subduing people and compelling them to accept a situation in which their freedom is being denied, along with their humanity, is a process far too complex and insidious to be the result of one mastermind alone. It is metonymical. There is a hierarchy that is built on mass acceptance of a certain language. The whole is represented in one image, while the one image takes on the larger meaning of the whole. In my lifetime, the oppressor was the State whose image was that of the tyrant Ceaușescu: the picture of the dictator was the very symbol of it. Nevertheless, the one man, Ceaușescu, could not have risen to power all by himself, and certainly could not have maintained himself in power alone. The figure of the State—of the communist State—on the other hand, is too vague in itself to carry any real power because there is no one specific, no one person in particular at whom to take aim. The State is an amorphous thing, 'the system'. We cannot visualize the millions who subscribe to the concept of one state over another, each one of the millions convinced by, and with his or her own private narrative on the matter. In our family's surveillance files I was able to find the components of the metonymy, the parts associated with and constructive of the whole that is oppression.

[31] Aristotle, *On Poetry and Style*, trans. G.M.A. Grube (Indianapolis: Hackett, 1958), p. 56.

In an oppressive regime, one person alone could have several identities at once, or could maintain just one: 'the informer', 'the card-carrying Party member', 'the bystander', 'the one who doesn't like to get involved', 'the profiteer', 'the dogmatic', 'the brainwashed', 'the victim', 'the docile citizen who obeys authority', 'the fervent believer', and as Stalin called writers, 'the engineers of the human soul'. It is difficult to ascertain who everyone was at the time of my father's protest against Ceaușescu, but listening to his story in his own words, I have come to understand that oppression was taking place in my country at that time largely because of silence. I wrote the poem 'The demonstration'[32] to portray that understanding:

The demonstration

I remember the night my father left
Filling a bag with leaflets and tying the placards
On top of the car: 'We Demand the Trial of the Ceaușescu Family
For Crimes Against Humanity, Usury and Economic Downfall.'

I complained about the boiled cabbage.
Please come and lock the gates. Tell them nothing.
I fell asleep on the kitchen sofa listening to Radio Free Europe.

In Bucharest he placed the placards on the front and back of the car.
He drove through traffic on the main street.
People came out of the stores shouting.
Buses and trams stopped, emptied, let him pass.

He threw leaflets with the left hand, drove with the right hand.
Ah, it was glorious! The flag of his country draped round his chest.
The portrait of the dictator decorated with black ribbons.

[32] Carmen Bugan, *Crossing the Carpathians* (Manchester: Oxford Poets/Carcanet, 2004), p. 14.

In a hospital, Dad's only son was born –
Mother held his bluish body wrapped in white cloth
At the window.

Thousands saw him being pulled from the car.
Watched him between armed soldiers.
None of his countrymen said a word.

Unlike Milosz, I did not have to contend with the influence of
the communist doctrine on my way of thinking. I was too young
at the time of my father's working man's act of dissent. Instead,
oppression arrived in my life as the direct brute reality of inter-
rogations and of visiting my father in one of the most horrifying
prisons in my country. My resistance was also instinctual and had
something to do with survival: in my case though, it was the sim-
ple survival of the family as a cohesive unit of persons who had
nourished me before my father's arrest.

Conclusion: 'Fertile Ground'

Like many in the Cold War generation, my parents fought, lost,
and were exiled. I have become a writer whose work is deeply
rooted in their legacy. As much as a poet, concerned with the
lyrical movement of language, might be repulsed by political lan-
guage, this language must be reckoned with, creatively, for it is
part of reality. My prayer is that I can reach into the language of
poetry, where oppression and freedom can have a fair fight. I write
because it takes me to that part of myself which is most alive. I
believe that I can write myself free and I can see myself free in the
poetry of others. Like Milosz, I subscribe to the salvational goal of

poetry: poetry might not save nations or people, but it is perfectly able to sound out one cry for freedom at the time. My poetry rubs against political language—the language of oppression—almost the way the present rubs at memory. How I create with the friction between the language of oppression and lyric language is the subject of the next three chapters: on constructing a lyric speaker from a sense of identity that fuses the public and private; writing in a non-native language; and developing artistic/emotional distance from the material in order to transform it.

I conclude with a poem which returns to the self under pressure; it is called 'Fertile Ground'.[33] I think this poem also sounds deeps of nature, with the voice of a child who stands her ground in front of powerful men, and in this sense it pushes against repression and the oppressor, who at that time was the interrogator:

Fertile ground

I was pruning tomato plants when they came to search
For weapons in our garden;
They dug the earth under the chickens, bell peppers,
Tiny melons, dill, and horse radishes.

I cried over sliced eggplants
Made one with the dirt,
Over fresh-dug earth and morning glories.

Their shovels uncovered bottles
With rusted metal caps – sunflower cooking oil

---

[33] Ibid., p. 15.

My father kept for 'dark days', purchased in days equally dark.
Their eyes lit – everyone got a bottle or two –
A promise for their families' meals.

And when the oil spilled on the ground, shiny over crushed tomatoes
They asked me about weapons we might have kept.
'Oil', I said: 'You eat and live.
This alone makes one dangerous.'

2

THE 'LYRIC I'

Private and public narratives

Pablo Neruda gives an account of how 'poetry was born' in him, in a section entitled 'My First Poem' in his *Memoirs*. He makes a compelling case for poetry as an expression of emotion, in a language 'different' from the one he spoke 'every day': I would like to explore this definition throughout the following discussion. The main project set at the beginning of this book concerns finding ways to extend the 'lyric I' so that poetry can achieve its full expressive potential, as it incorporates the experience—and the language—of oppression. Here I reflect on the poet's identity (shaped by experience) and on the poet-speaker (a linguistic construct involving authorial intent and the reader) in the context of political oppression and state surveillance. The distinctions between the private and the public aspects of the self will play out in the discussion of subject matter and style, and the role of self-expression in literature, especially as it concerns the poet's inner freedom. The reflections on the experience of oppression enter the speaking voice in the poems naturally as part of the poet's lived life, as there is no such thing as separation from one's own experience. One's emotions and beliefs are synthesized into a unified whole, which is the poem on the page. All these issues come

Poetry and the Language of Oppression: Essays on Politics and Poetics. Carmen Bugan, Oxford University Press (2021). © Carmen Bugan. DOI: 10.1093/oso/9780198868323.003.0003

together as the 'lyric I' (through which the voice of the poet is being heard) comes into being and evolves.

Neruda says that when he wrote his first poem he 'felt an intense emotion and set down a few words, half-rhymed but strange to me, different from everyday language'. He offered the poem to his 'angelic stepmother whose gentle shadow watched' over his childhood. He locates the birth of poetry in intense emotion. He recounts his initial understanding of poetic language as something 'strange' and identifies a specific recipient for the gift of this transformed language. But he opens this section with a story about a swan, which to me reads as an indication of another component of poetry: the poet's individual understanding of the received truths about the larger world, so essential in establishing the voice of the poet-speaker. Though the poet might speak about his private experience, he does so within the hearing of others and as making a gift to them. This story often comes to mind when I think about the triangle of the self, experience, and lyric language:

> Someone brought me a swan that was half dead. It was one of those magnificent birds I have not seen again anywhere in the world, a black-necked swan. A snowy vessel with its slender neck looking as if squeezed into a black silk stocking, its beak an orange color and its eyes red.
>
> This happened at the seaside, in Puerto Saavedra, Imperial del Sur.
>
> It was almost dead when they gave it to me. I bathed its wounds and stuffed bits of bread and fish down its throat. It threw up everything. But it recovered from its injuries gradually and began to realize that I was its friend. And I began to realize that homesickness was killing it. So I went down the streets to the river, with the heavy bird in my arms. It swam a little way, close by. I wanted it to fish and showed it pebbles on the bottom, the sand and silver fish of the south were gliding over. But its sad eyes wandered off in the distance.

I carried it to the river and back to my house every day for more than twenty days. The swan was almost as tall as me. One afternoon it seemed dreamier; it swam near me but wasn't entertained by my ruses for trying to teach it how to fish again. It was very still and I picked it up in my arms to take it home. But when I held it up to my breast, I felt a ribbon unrolling, and something like a black arm brushed my face. It was the long, sinuous neck falling. That's how I found out that swans don't sing when they die.[1]

The story is about Neruda's younger self making a failed attempt at healing an injured swan which was given to him. There are similes—the swan's neck is a ribbon, it is squeezed into a black stocking, it is like a black arm—that help build elaborate human imagery, so that the swan becomes a metaphor expressing a larger, inevitable human loss. That Neruda places this memory in a section entitled his 'first poem' is suggestive: he intimates the origins of his lyric speaker in his own self actively engaging with the wider world. In the context of a memoir about writing, this is a story about the poet's first encounter with the world as it had been passed on to him, and to which he became deeply attached, at least momentarily believing he could heal it. The account of this memory gives us a perspective on the poetry he wrote later on 'for the people'. What we create as art—the public utterance we make—is born in us, more precisely in our interaction with our environment, which is often a coincidence of geography, history, and language. Twenty days carrying the swan to the river to teach it to live again, its dreaminess, the sense almost of a ritual act, the moving observation that he and the swan were about the same size—showing feelings of identification—the transformation, the

---

[1] Pablo Neruda, *Memoirs*, trans. Hardie St. Martin (London: Souvenir Press, 2004), pp. 18–20.

bitter wisdom, all individual and private rites of passage: they are Neruda's poem as he explains it to us. We can sense his desire to understand and name the experience. We can see him challenging the received knowledge that swans sing before they die, by offering his own experience as disproof. At the end of the final sentence we are left with that pain in the pit of our stomach, because we too understand something fundamental about loss, or because we are reminded of loss in our own lives.

Neruda's story appeals to me because it feels immediately recognizable as an expression of our natural instinct as it guides our communion with the world. The poet inherits an injured world with which he identifies and which he learns that he cannot save. Nevertheless he offers himself and his soothing words to it, both because the world awakens in him feelings of compassion and because poetry makes it possible to express himself in a moving way. In the making of the poem there enter one's self, experience, and one's hope in a capacious sense: they enliven language. The questions follow: how is the 'lyric I' made and how does it stand on the ball of its foot, like a ballerina, balancing what is within and what is without, so that each movement in language is not only graceful but ripe with deep meaning, with that echo of recognition? More importantly, how is language put at the service of life?

Defining the 'Lyric I'

I would like to keep Neruda's account of beginning to write poetry as a point of reference throughout the following discussion on how political oppression influences a poet's voice, because I think the principle of locating the 'lyric I' is the same, regardless of the context in which we write. The poetry that originates in political oppression follows the natural cycle of birth and expression like all other lyric poetry: it still originates in intense emotion, it still voices the poet's gained knowledge of the world, it is still a language different from everyday speech, and it is still an offering to the reader. The difference lies in the particulars of experience with which it engages and the particular everyday language which it resists. For one thing, the experience of oppression heightens the poet's sensitivity to suffering and to language: one is on constant alert for threats. This heightened sensitivity enters the voice of the poet-speaker naturally and spontaneously, determining the emotional character of his or her poetic language. In addition, engaging with injustice imparts another, more public, quality to the writing that brings its own set of concerns: the poem moves from being a strictly private expression to one that incorporates public unease, since the oppression internalized is of public provenance. The 'lyric I' is the expressive entity located between the poet's biographical self and the world of readers. In some sense it represents the poet's essential connection with language. Its voice sounds out the poet's language, which is inherited and cared for in much the same way as Neruda's swan.

I wanted to start with an insistence on the individual, the particular, the emotional, and the subjective because most poets do not embrace language in order to write national anthems, protest marching songs, or to represent an abstract humanity. But the poet who sees or experiences injustice, and sees greed ruling the law, sees people suffering, cannot turn away because such things do not offer an 'aesthetic experience' or because such experiences are antithetical to 'beautiful language'. Like everyone else alive, the poet belongs to the world and is moved and transformed by it. While it is true that in telling a story one doesn't tell them all, it is also true that in voicing a lament, a grief about the state of the world, the poet becomes attuned to and expresses his or her sense of 'public emotion'. The expression of the particular is certainly not the expression of the universal: yet it is part of it. It's important to make the point here that, in this context, 'authorial intent' has to do with clarity of expression—knowing what one says and being responsible for how it is articulated—rather than 'intent' in the sense of aiming to create an *effect* on the reader. The poet controls the making of the poem, but cannot truly know how the poem is being read, interpreted, and felt.

There are various theories about the place of experience in poetry and in art in general. Experience is the primary way of understanding the world around us, as it involves close observation, perceiving the reality with one's senses, and engaging with that information by more abstract means, such as reflection and contemplation. Creative experience comes with practice that perfects representations of life as seen and understood by the artist. In his *Notebooks*, Leonardo da Vinci praises experience in terms which bring to mind the idea of artistic self-reliance: 'my works are the issue of simple and plain experience which is the true mistress'. To him, 'All our knowledge has its origins in our perceptions.' Da Vinci argues that our 'senses are of the earth' and that 'reason stands apart from them in contemplation'.[2] The artist, and, to me, this is the poet, begins with these primary ingredients, which through the creative process—essentially interpretive— achieve expression. Expression is the union of the mind and the

---

[2] Leonardo da Vinci, *Notebooks*, sel., Irma A. Richter; ed., Thereza Wells (Oxford: Oxford University Press, 2008), pp. 3, 6, 7.

senses. According to da Vinci, 'the actions of the figures are in every case expressive of the purpose of their minds' so that the figure 'most worthy of praise' is the one 'which by its action best expresses the passion which animates it'. Both maker and audience are moved by artistic expression instinctually: 'The lover is moved by things loved, as the sense is by that which it perceives, and it unites with it and they become one and the same thing. The work is the first thing born of the union.' [3] When the union of the mind and the senses takes place—through the process of perfecting the craft—the poem, like the painting, becomes memorable: what the 'lyric I' animates, even as it arises from a specific time, takes its place outside that time, entering into the time of humanity.

The role of experience in literature (and poetry more specifically) also concerns the value we place on listening to each other's stories. The experience presented in poetry (life experiences, observations on people and the events that affect them, character studies, one's sense of truth, etc.) may have a 'didactic' purpose, awakening the reader to the dynamic relationship between choices and consequences, but poets need to be somewhat wary of this view. The idea of the poet as a representative of the 'republic of conscience' leads to expectations of 'socially-conscious poetry' or a 'poetry of social justice' which can easily turn the genre into a political or sociological tool. Though clearly engaging with true events, poetry does not offer the type of account that replaces journalism, legal testimony, or researched historical accounts with an emotionally eloquent persuasion about the truth. Poetry gives us an account of what it *feels* like to have lived in a specific place at a particular time, experiencing certain events,

[3] Ibid., pp. 168–9.

or a retrospective account of what it was like to have been there. Accurate and truthful to facts as it *must* be, it is one individual experience of history. The weight of the narrative is on feeling and perception, opening a space for the reader; it aims to pose questions such as 'What is love?', 'What is freedom?', 'What is solitude?' A rendering of experience in poetry is both indispensable as a window into another's life, and absolutely useless as a testimony for politicians and policy-makers who are looking for perpetrators, victims, demagogical spin-offs, and compensations. Viewed in this way, the poem opens a moral, contemplative space for the reader, rather than teaching the reader 'how to behave morally'. At its most ambitious, the poem, like a proverb, a riddle, or a fable, takes the reader from one moral position and leaves him or her in another. It is specifically in this way that the poet who has experienced oppression can claim the right to speak out: what we should be interested in is the effects of oppression on the human soul, rather than chasing the oppressor for revenge. The intervention happens first in self-healing, then in opening avenues to other worlds for the reader, letting the reader travel those worlds.

It is for this reason that it is possible to say, with Auden, that 'poetry makes nothing happen' (in both senses of causing no empirical changes, and bringing what was nothing into virtual existence), while at the same time insisting on its vital presence in our lives.[4] The truth of poetry lies in its ability to bring to the mind of the reader something deeply felt by the poet, and deeply expressed in language. The depth of expression makes the experience memorable. So, though clearly capable of engaging with

---

[4] W.H. Auden, 'In Memory of W.B. Yeats', in *Selected Poems*, ed. Edward Mandelson (London: Faber and Faber, 1979), p. 80.

factual historical traumas that affect large segments of the population, poetry is about the life of the mind. The poem is offered to the reader as a gift, for whatever pleasure or use, in the same way a flower blossoms by the side of the road for anyone who might pass it. The bearer of the poem is the 'lyric I' which is born of the poet's experience and has the task of making that truthful person-to-person communication possible.

The Individual, the State, and the Poet-speaker

The spontaneous offering of language from heart to heart does not absolve the poet of responsibilities. Where does this sense of responsibility come from? Unlike the flower which is an expression of nature, the poem is a deliberate construction in language, obeying conventions that are constantly learned, debated, and reinvented. The question posed above has to do with the reader, who will sense the expressive characteristics of the language. The reader will 'receive' the poetry according to his or her sensibilities and cultural expectations, whether the poem is a form of self-absorbed self-reflection, or whether it is an earnest effort to commune with the language and its speakers, or, more ambitiously, to expose injustice. In poetry about historical events and moments of public trauma, whether the poet likes it or not, the work will be understood, at least to some extent, as a 'topical' representation, the public trauma itself understood, in turn, through the language of the poetry that renders it. But to what extent does the poet speak *for* the community of readers? What is meant by 'language and its speakers' and what does it mean to 'commune with' them? It is here that we run into the debate about the subjective vs. the objective and the question of whether the particular represents the universal.

The perception of particular as universal has to do, I believe, with how we understand ourselves in relation to the world: whether our sense of identity is entirely derived from society (therefore, we speak as one of many), or whether each of us is an entirely separate strand—essential to making up the fabric and its durability, and yet perfectly detachable from it (therefore, we speak as a unique individual). The question was pondered by Jean-Jacques Rousseau in *The Social Contract*, where he argued for a system of organizing society successfully, taking 'men as they are and laws as they might be' in such a way as to preserve the maximum freedom possible for the individual 'so that justice and utility are in no way divided'.[5] In his own words, Rousseau asked: 'How to find a form of association which will defend the person and goods of each member with the collective force of all, and under which each individual, while uniting himself with the others, obeys no one but himself, and remains as free as before?'[6] By subscribing to a social contract, an individual exchanges 'natural independence for freedom'.[7] Renouncing the 'natural liberty'—the freedom to rely solely on the self for protection and comfort—in order to become a member of 'civil society' gives one 'civil liberty' and 'moral freedom' by which all individual actions gain moral significance.[8] This makes the solitary individual 'a part of a much greater whole, from which that same individual will then receive,

---

[5] Jean-Jacques Rousseau, *The Social Contract*, trans. Maurice Cranston (London: Penguin Books, 1968), p. 1.

[6] Ibid., p. 14.

[7] Ibid., p. 36.

[8] Ibid., p. 21.

in a sense, his life and his being'. One becomes a citizen—a public construct of identity by which one is compelled to subscribe to, and participate in, the republic (the larger community), tying the individual inextricably with others in a 'communal existence'.[9]

But how are we to decide what constitutes personal freedom and what constitutes a series of concessions by which conformity replaces that sense of well-being that can only be achieved when one is entirely in charge of one's own destiny? I have in mind here the sense of freedom as Jack London's 'sheer surging of life',[10] which I discussed in Chapter 1. This question requires answering a deeper one first: what is individual humanity and what is common humanity and in terms of which do we understand ourselves? Rousseau cites Grotius's dilemma of 'whether humanity belongs to a hundred men, or whether these hundred men belong to humanity',[11] leaving us with very little room to believe that we can somehow live outside of society or even imagine ourselves outside of it. We are born both as private and as public people, even though we are only aware of ourselves in the privacy of the family at first. It follows that we understand ourselves in terms of both.

The idea of being both independent and yet entirely subscribed to one's society has challenged poets throughout history and has led to the various positions which they adopted: 'the outsider', 'the prophet', 'the Poet Laureate', 'the sage'. The rift between the self and the crowd, especially in dysfunctional societies, has also affected common citizens like my father, who was caught between a commitment to the safety of his family and a moral

---

[9] Ibid., pp. 44–5.
[10] Jack London, *The Call of the Wild* (London: Puffin Books, 1982, 2015), p. 46
[11] Rousseau, *The Social Contract*, p. 4.

imperative to decry injustice. Finally, it also challenges me both as a citizen and as a poet, who has left a society where a person's value was based on contributing to the community and blending in, and entered a society where one's value is judged on the ability to stand out from the crowd. During the past thirty years I have come full circle on the question of where the individual is placed in society, whether humanity belongs to one person or whether one person belongs to humanity, and whether poetry can truly voice a sense of belonging to one culture or another.

Since my work is concerned with government oppression and its impact on family, it is necessary to define government, before considering the role of language and the 'lyric I' in this context. I believe that the government determines an individual's course of existence and thus influences the construction of the poet-speaker, whose voice is born from an understanding of values such as freedom. According to Rousseau, the government is 'a body charged with the execution of the laws and the maintenance of freedom, both civil and political'.[12] Citizens form a body politic that is directed by the government, which will 'do for the public person what is done for the individual by the union of soul and body'.[13] The imagery of 'body and soul' invoked by Rousseau makes it clear that the individual can only perceive the self as part of the community. The awareness of such dependency—in two different political systems—has been crucial to my own life and my writing, and I know it will preoccupy me for the rest of my life. My work harks for independence: at the moment it still defines itself either in terms of or against a political system. I think it is

[12] Ibid., p. 65.
[13] Ibid., p. 65.

impossible to define ourselves as independent of the forces in our societies, regardless of being marginalized for our lack of conformity to them. Like all poets who sought political refuge from an oppressive government, I struggle with full self-identification with, and acceptance into, the welcoming other.

Language plays a major role in artistic self-definition, rendering clarity to the 'lyric I' which voices certain aspects of the human condition. I will devote Chapter 3 to the discussion of writing in a non-native language and identifying with a community of readers. For now, I want to delve a bit deeper into the subject of how we understand our human condition, and whether that understanding gives us a stronger sense of independence. John Stuart Mill argued two things which are important to me here. One is about the human character and developing a sense of morality, and the other is about the character of the poet in particular:

> The human faculties of perception, judgement, discriminative feeling, mental activity, and even moral preference are exercised only in making a choice. He who does anything because it is the custom makes no choice. He gains no practice either in discerning or in desiring what is best. The mental and moral, like the muscular powers, are improved only by being used...
>
> He who chooses his plan for himself employs all his faculties. He must use observation to see, reasoning and judgement to foresee, activity to gather material for decision, discrimination to decide, and when he has decided, firmness and self-control to hold to his deliberate decision.[14]

---

[14] John Stuart Mill, 'On Liberty', in *The Norton Anthology of English Literature*, Sixth edition, ed., M.H. Abrams (New York: W.W.W. Norton, 1993), p. 1004.

Tremendous emphasis is placed on the individual here: it involves self-reliance, independence in exercising choices, developing an ability to discern and to see the world with lucidity. In a sense, Mill's 'art of living' resembles da Vinci's 'art of painting' where, in Mill's words, 'To give any fair play to the nature of each, it is essential that different persons should be allowed to lead different lives.'[15] One embraces the union of experience, feelings, and reason. One lives actively rather than passively. In order to achieve this, it is crucial to discern between the concessions necessary to be part of society and the passivity of social conformity. I believe this specific independence of the self is absolutely necessary in order to articulate a strong poetic speaking voice, which expresses the self in relation to the world. About the figure of the poet, John Stuart Mill said:

> But poetry, which is the delineation of the deeper and more secret workings of human emotion, is interesting only to those to whom it recalls what they have felt, or whose imagination it stirs up to conceive what they could feel, or what they might have been able to feel, had their outward circumstances been different.
>
> …What they [the poets] know has come by observation of themselves: they have found within them one highly delicate and sensitive specimen of human nature, on which the laws of emotion are written in large characters, such as can be read off without much study.[16]

---

[15] Ibid., p. 1007.
[16] John Stuart Mill, 'What Is Poetry?', in *The Norton Anthology of English Literature*, Sixth edition, ed., M.H. Abrams (New York: W.W.W. Norton, 1993), p. 996.

Again, we are reminded of da Vinci's reflections on how art communicates: on that ability to make itself recognized by others' senses. Mill's valuation of poetry is determined by poetry's ability to communicate emotion in such a way that the readers are reminded of what they themselves have felt, or in such a way that it stimulates their imagination to 'conceive' feelings they had not felt before. In other words, poetry is good if it opens the reader to other worlds or if it opens those other worlds to the reader. To master this, the first book the poet must read is that of oneself: there, one will find 'the laws of emotion'.

Matthew Arnold wrote still more deeply about the character of the poet and the poet's place in the world:

> The grand power of poetry is its interpretative power; by which I mean, not a power of drawing out in black and white an explanation of the mystery of the universe, but the power of so dealing with things as to awaken in us a wonderfully full, new, and intimate sense of them, and of our relations with them ...
>
> I have said that poetry interprets in two ways; it interprets by expressing, with magical felicity, the physiognomy and movement of the outward world, and it interprets by expressing, with inspired conviction, the ideas and laws of the inward world of man's moral and spiritual nature. In other words, poetry is interpretative both by having *natural magic* in it, and by having *moral profundity*. In both ways it illuminates man; it gives him a satisfying sense of reality; it reconciles him with himself and the universe.[17]

It is precisely in this sense that the 'lyric I' must be expanded, especially as it expresses the experience of oppression. The

---

[17] Matthew Arnold, 'Maurice de Guerin: A Definition of Poetry', in *The Norton Anthology of English Literature*, Sixth edition, ed., M.H. Abrams (New York: W.W.W. Norton, 1993), p. 1403.

subject matter, oppression, must be rendered in such a way as to 'awaken in us' the 'intimate sense' of that experience, rather than giving the reader a 'drawing out in black and white' of it. No poet can speak convincingly or truthfully unless he or she is wholly himself or herself. Each of us experiences beauty, terror, freedom, and justice on our own terms. Individuality, moral profundity, observation, and compassion—these are the ways to extend the 'lyric I' in order to press against suppression and oppression. That 'lyric I' needs to be inside the heart of the girl who receives death threats from the parents of her friend, and it has to feel what the girl feels. It has to know how to handle itself. But then what happens when one is not entirely free—has suppressed parts of the self, as a victim of oppression—and writes *in order to* discover and claim personal freedom? This is a question for all the writers who have had a background of oppression, slavery, have experienced the horrors of mass migrations, or have suffered abuse.

Poetry from Inhuman Places

I would like to offer a story about a private family moment which had been recorded, transcribed, archived, and kept as a public document. It is a story about exposure and identity, which to me poses the questions of how to respond to the language of surveillance and how to write from a sense of violation. When he was released from prison in 1988, my father was recorded by the microphones installed by the Securitate in our bedroom, while he was reciting a revolutionary poem by George Coşbuc to my young brother. Here is the transcript, which for the time being, will take the place of Neruda's swan:

Date: February 12, 1988
'Barbu'
('In attention')

Hour 6:00, in the room the obj. listens to the news from Radio Free Europe.

The children sleep, he is listening by himself.

At 7:35 Carmen leaves the house…

The obj. is reciting the following verses to his son:

"Let us not by the will of the Holy God
Crave blood, instead of land.
When we will reach the end of patience,
Everything, by turn, will end."

Son: Is this all?
Obj.: Eh! I no longer know this poem…I would like to live alone,
    not with people, because I do not trust them.
Son: Is this the meaning of loneliness?
Obj.: Yes.

The writing in this document is illuminating: it gives access to an intimate moment of family life, and it is framed in a language that somehow makes this moment a matter of formal political inquiry. On 12 February 1988, seven days after my father was freed from the Aiud prison following the General Amnesty issued by Ceaușescu, there was a conversation between him and my younger brother Cătălin, who was 5 years old at the time. I read the transcription of this conversation for the first time in 2013. My father is designated by the word *obiectiv*, or 'object', literally meaning 'the object of observation': he is abbreviated to 'obj.'. The title of the file, 'Barbu,' is a codename sometimes used for my mother, sometimes used for my father, and sometimes used for distinguishing the recordings made in our house from those made in other places, such as the homes of relatives and friends. The note at the top of the page, 'In attention', indicates that some official was particularly interested in this material. There are additional numbers given at the top of the original document indicating the type of recording made and how it was archived. The dates of the recording and its transcription are also given.

Aside from the aspect that this is an observation log of the activity taking place in the house such as my father listening to the illegal Radio Free Europe at six in the morning, us being asleep, then me leaving the house, this document interests me because it reveals, or creates a sense of the relationship between my brother and my father, as well as a psychological portrait of my father. Could this be construed as a form of biography? After all, it aims to present the reader (the high-ranked secret police staff) with an accurate portrait. In the context of return from prison, this conversation can be read as a monologue of Dad's first thoughts about being 'free'. My little brother is too young to fully understand the meaning of the words he hears. My father struggles with the tension between wanting to be gentle and feeling that he could no longer trust anyone. He talks to Cătălin as if he is talking aloud to himself. He recites a poem, perhaps out of a desire to be like the other fathers reading stories to their young children.

Yet the poem, written by the celebrated George Coşbuc (1866–1918) is a vatic piece that is firmly rooted in the Romanian poetic and indeed, revolutionary, imagination. It appears in other files where my father expresses anger at the political system, symbolizing thus, at least in the context of my family life, rebellion.

'Noi vrem pamint' [We want our land][18] illustrates the depth of the relationship between the dispossessed Romanian peasant and his native soil; it is one of the literary masterpieces that chronicle the spirit of the bloody 1907 Peasant Uprising, when people went hungry while tilling the soil of the landowners. The first line is a prayer that God should not allow anger—a thirst for bloodshed. The last two lines warn that when people reach the end of patience, only destruction will come. Rereading the entire poem now, I see why it captured my father's imagination: like the peasants who worked and couldn't feed themselves off the land, he was not allowed to work and feed himself off his native soil. He rebelled against hunger, and was punished. Remarkably, like all great literature that transcends its own historical time, the poem captures the spirit of two moments of social duress: the pre-communist era and the high communist violation of human rights, though, ironically, the Ceaușescu propaganda machine had also used this poem to exalt the virtues of the resilient, hard-working peasants. But my father does not remember the whole poem and abandons it.

At this point the voice of the trusting son breaks in with life-fresh curiosity. Cătălin asks Dad: 'Is this all?' He wants to know more. He slips into the mode of the story time, one he knows from being with my mother and us, his two sisters. He expects Dad to continue. My father shrugs the poem off but in a remark filled with what I expect to be the weight of the lines he had just recited, confesses to his son, 'I want to live alone, not with people, because I do not trust them.' My father still wants to live, which is important. But he no longer wants to be among people, having

[18] George Coșbuc, 'Noi Vrem Pamint', https://www.versuri.ro/versuri/george-Coșbuc-noi-vrem-pamant-_u217.html.

seen the worst side of them. He is an outcast. Most likely the literal marks of the prison chains are still on his wrists and his ankles as he recites this poem to my brother. And yet, as I see it now, the saving grace of my father's words is that they are brimming with *feeling*, and with poetry. This is the tiny door that opens to me and my work as a poet—now, once again, as back then in 1983 and 1984 when I was writing poems to his picture, which was framed in the hallway, the back of the picture itself bruised by the blades of the secret police knives, as they stripped it from the frame during the house search, when I was 12 years old.

Cătălin rescues my father with his innocence. He wants to name what my father feels and asks a practical question: 'Is this the meaning of loneliness?' He is a 5-year old learning a word the other way around: from denotation and connotation to the actual word. My father teaches him, unwillingly, what is meant by loneliness, and Cătălin almost finds the word for it in his vocabulary. In school it would have been the case that a word would be written on the board—'loneliness', for example—and then the teacher would give an appropriate explanation of it, maybe something like 'a little bear with no friends is lonely'. The vocabulary lesson would start from the word: from the abstract. But here the lesson starts from feeling—from the concrete— and moves towards the word. It is an experiential learning of language. I believe this kind of learning takes place at moments of great trial in our lives, when we reach for words to articulate the burden of what we feel. Language, at such times, becomes rooted in the concrete, the real, the deep experience of life, gaining an invaluable verisimilitude with that which it voices. My brother must have known the word at that age because he must have heard us saying it around the house, but it seems extraordinary to me that he put it together with my father's experience in the context of that conversation.

Did the secret police want to portray my father as a broken man? As a person who is angry and ready to rebel again? Or did they want to show him as someone unstable, saying inappropriate and hurtful things to his son, such as giving the idea that he doesn't want to be with our family? Who knows? What I can tell from the language is that the agent-narrator looks on the scene of the room with clinical coldness and separates the dialogue from his own observations. As a piece of writing, this is a testimony of an admission of having given up on society (represented by my father's words), and the thirst for life and learning (as represented by my brother's). Despair and hope lived with each other in our home and in our hearts: so did the oppressor.

I don't see this document as an isolated piece of my family's history; I see it as expressing the struggles that take place in our souls when history forces us to deal with evil. The fact that the Securitate had free and complete access to such an intimate and painful conversation is a reminder that individual people are powerless and transparent when they are placed under the eye of tyranny. It is also a directive to me, the poet, the writer, to use the resources of the free language in exacting ways, to be direct and honest in acknowledging both pain and the blessings of language available to me—of the languages available to me—in order to bring out the necessary testimony of hope.

The speaker of a poem makes a public utterance, in the formal language of poetry, about a personal, private feeling. That 'I' is a construction that reflects the authorial figure, the personal biography, and the values (public, family, literary) assumed to be held by the readers.

But when the poet's own sense of self is destabilized because there is a version of that self out there that has been produced by the State, then one has trouble constructing a unified, harmonious voice for the 'I' that speaks as one's self in history. The secret police account of my activity as a child in Romania is troubling in the sense that I have no memory of certain events that have been recorded as having taken place. While I feel fine as a person who has suffered memory loss, how am I supposed to deal with seeing myself as a character in someone else's official version of my life which I cannot verify? More troubling still is to read accounts of events that have taken place in my family while I was absent, and which give me new ways to look at 'us'.

In the light of my reading of these files, I wonder what language should become in my own hands. Should it be an instrument used to blame communism, surveillance, totalitarianism? Should the poetry become more publicly a voice against injustice? My responsibility towards my family was to acknowledge loss and absence, and then to fill the empty space with memories where we could be together, at least in my words. It was the best I could do, and it worked. The poems remained focused on the particulars of our situation, rather than turning into a howl of protest, which would have done nothing other than terrify my mother and sister, who already were afraid to read the poems aloud. It is in this process that I found my voice. Reading the outsider's view on the life of the child I was, requires lyrical readjustment.

The poet who is a victim engages directly with oppression in order to rid his or her private language of it, and looks at the lyric language as something which inevitably treats politics, and political oppression as experience. The fine tuning of the 'lyric I'—the decisions made on who speaks and from what kind of experience—is my concern here, because this lyric speaker has an identity that fuses the public and private. The aim is to seek to unify the public and the private against destabilizing forces, so that the voice of the 'lyric I' is whole, managing to speak to the individual and to the larger culture, remaining emotionally, intellectually, and artistically comprehensible to both. Poetry explores the large territory of feelings and probes its edges, the places of rupture, the fault lines, the fissures in the landscape—in order to learn about the movement of the tectonic plates that uphold the logic of its continents. The poet learns how the large tectonic plates of feelings—love, pity, hatred, and grief—shift, in order to both explain and predict their movement. In addition, the poet also has to work to actually help shift the feelings (his or her own first) by using the imagination as that liminal space where the movement from grief towards healing takes place. In the act of reading the poem, the reader can reach beyond what is known and predictable. This requires a clarity of purpose. The 'I' of the poet who writes a personal testimony is not a dramatic persona used as a vehicle to stand for something, stand against something, comment on something, or ascertain greater truths, and it is not a mask. This 'lyric I' of personal testimony is a much humbler construction. One's artistic obligation is to make art of the real subject matter, and to speak as one's self. We must use the primary ingredients of lived life in the construction of the 'lyric I'. This is a strength. Constructing the 'lyric I' in this manner leads to writing as a public confession, rather than simply a public expression, though expression it is.

The speaker in the following poem, 'Portrait of a family',[19] written years after surveillance, in another language, doubts the ability of the lyric language to heal the damage the State inflicted on the family, and yet at the same time shows the language following and recording the family. When I wrote this poem, I seriously doubted my skills to put right the experience of those years. I wanted to protect our privacy as a family and yet talk about everything at the same time, with the voice of a family member who walks around the house trying to soothe the others. I am glad the doubt has remained: doubting keeps us safe from complacency. The 'lyric I' here is a clearly involved observer, who sees the house, the garden, the people in the house, the woman in the hospital, the prison, and also the language that has become people:

Portrait of a family

When the strangers walked into the house,
Took the paintings off the walls, and
Sealed off the rooms with red wax,

Part of this poem listened in a hospital. A woman's milk
Fed the words she couldn't say into her child's mouth.
For seven months the strangers stayed in the house.

Someone tied the hands of the man
Who inflamed the centre of the capital with protest
While they took the paintings off the walls.

A few lines cowered in the grass, outside the windows,
With the neighbours who watched the girl answering questions
To the strangers who settled into the house.

[19] Carmen Bugan, 'Portrait of a Family', in *Crossing the Carpathians* (Manchester: Oxford Poets/Carcanet, 2004), p. 13.

And yet someone followed her sister on the streets
And photographed her pure black eyes,
Unsuspecting in the paintings on the walls.

Now that the strangers have left the house
The poem would like to know:
Can it place once more the paintings on the walls,

Will the son tell the secrets of his mother's milk,
Will the handcuffs come off the man's hands,
Will the girl stop answering questions,
Will her sister burn the photographs?

The voice I adopt in the poetry dealing with the language of the files has a grain of the 'outsider looking in', which destabilizes the straightforward lyrical voice of a self, painting an emotional scene as an 'insider looking out'. It expresses the distance in time and experience from those years of surveillance through the point of view of someone who has also known a different life. Having absorbed the voice of the secret police transcribers into my own writing voice, I feel at times that there is an 'other' narrator that interjects into the poems.

Conclusion: Poetry as a Gift

In my own work, I feel that poetry must 'act' on the sense of family as a social microcosm, it must dwell where the battle between the public self and the private self takes place: it is a battle because that 'public self' Rousseau talks about has become for me a 'secret police document' rather than a citizen who truly belonged to the body politic. Focusing on the story of family, and the individual under political duress, helped me put a human face on suffering, a face that I hope will forever shine against 'the obj.'. I wrote the poem entitled 'We are museums'[20] to express the experience of personal violation because of government surveillance:

We are museums

We have now become museums. The inside of our souls
Was turned out like the lining of coats hung to dry,
And our souls have dried. Out of us came the warm breath
That you see when you blow on a window or in winter air.

Out of our footprints through the town, from the sound
Of us walking around the house they have made maps.
When we stopped at a shop window, the minutes were noted,
The address and what we looked at were kept on record:

The red dress on a mannequin, empty shelves in a bakery
On Hope, Victory, or People Street. Because we have become
'Objects of observation', 'targets', since nothing more has remained
Of the people we were, we are now museums.

On the ground level where we are closest to the earth, you will find
Our house and garden, fruit trees and sparrows, nightingales
And monarch butterflies. Then came the time of upheaval when birds
Were shooed from branches where microphones were installed.

The dog was poisoned by informers and the child was recorded
On a tape, when the electricity was on. The end of the girl's first love,
Her angry letters have rooms of their own, furnished with her mother's
Sympathy: maybe they were kept to indict us for having had feelings?

There are records of us eating sour soup and polenta, drinking linden tea,
Mother knitting sweaters at two in the morning to exchange for eggs
And flour; you will find her sitting on the bed 'alone by herself
Talking to no one for many hours,' framed forever in the state archives.

---

[20] Carmen Bugan, 'We are museums', in *Releasing the Porcelain Birds: Poems after Surveillance* (Swindon: Shearsman, 2016), p. 11.

On the top floor, where we are further up from the earth, you will see us
Trying to escape: the girl asks her father to 'please talk about Kant',
And he says 'plan to live without me if I am assassinated'. We are
Museums. I am writing this down so you can come inside us to see.

There are no secrets anyway, everything about us has been recorded:
Night dreams and rage, irony and double-meaning, shopping we did
At the pharmacy, tears on our cheeks, even the illusion that
There might have been *something* we could have kept for ourselves.

(February–April 2013)

When I explain where I come from, I sometimes say that in 1984, when I was 14 years old, I lived in a situation similar to the one imagined by George Orwell in his novel, *1984*. The early experience of totalitarianism has determined the course of my writing life. But researching the secret police archives of my family life, a quarter century after the surveillance had ended and we had left the country, changed the voice of the poet I had built in exile. There are two versions of personal identity that often clash in the artistic process originating in oppression: the identity before oppression, and the one developed as a response to oppression. They destabilize the voice of the 'lyric I'.

This quest for unity in the 'lyric I' brings to mind the Russian poet Osip Mandelstam, who brought together the chaos of his personal life under Stalin's tyranny into a tremendously strong and unified lyric speaker. In the Introduction to his book, *A Coat of Many Colors: Osip Mandelstam and His Mythologies of Self-Presentation*, the critic Gregory Freidin explains his fascination with the figure of the Russian poet as follows:

> He worked consistently at designing a figure that could serve as a unifying epic or dramatic center for a variety of lyric gestures. He was thus able to satisfy a major condition for being a lyric poet in

contemporary Russia, namely, to compose poetry capable of projecting a powerful, integrative self. Such a self had to be grounded not only in the particular circumstances and consciousness of the poet as an individual but also in the consciousness of the audience; in short, in the culture of the body social to which the poet appealed. Furthermore, the self had to be flexible, able to respond to the rapidly changing world, yet stable enough to remain recognizable, allowing the poet to maintain narrative continuity in self-presentation.[21]

My fascination with Mandelstam and poets like him who had remained in their countries, or were exiled but retained their love and faith in their native language, has to do with my choice to abandon my native language altogether. Many poets could not be separated from their language, whereas I found comfort in leaving it behind, only to find myself haunted by a different set of questions regarding 'the culture and body social' where my work might seek readership. That is the subject of Chapter 3.

I want to return to the notion of poetry as a gift. There is a wonderful poem by R.S. Thomas called 'Gifts',[22] which could be read both literally and as a poetics. The gifts the poet inherited were: a 'strong heart' and a 'weak stomach' from his father, 'fear' from his mother, and 'shame' from his country. And when it came time to think about the gifts he would bestow on his own family, he chose 'all' he had for his wife, and his 'hunger' for his son. R.S. Thomas takes things further than Neruda. He positions himself in between generations. As with all great literature, there is a generous space between each line of the poem, where the reader can insert his or

---

[21] Gregory Freidin, A Coat of Many Colors: Osip Mandelstam and His Mythologies of Self-Presentation (Berkeley: University of California Press, 2010), p. X.

[22] R.S. Thomas, Collected Poems 1945–1990 (London: Orion/Phoenix Books, 2000), p. 161.

her own version of inheritance and legacy. What have I received from my mother? What have I received from my father? What have I received from my country? What do I give my children, my spouse? 'To my one son the hunger', he says. What kind of hunger? That is for the reader to imagine. Yet, as with Neruda, everything remains in the earthly, and earthy. The extraordinary simplicity and lucidity of these pieces tell me that these poets, and their lyric speakers know themselves to the core.

Having endured tyranny doesn't make *anyone* a poet: but making tyranny understood by others, making it present in the minds of others, and finding the language that helps to keep it out, *does*. I believe that the 'lyric I' has the task of looking clearly for as long and as deep as it takes into the experience of oppression in order to understand it and set it aside, bitterness and chains and all. I return to da Vinci once again, this time on government: 'When besieged by ambitious tyrants I find a means of offence and defence in order to preserve the chief gift of nature, which is liberty; and first I would speak of the position of the walls, and then of how the various peoples can maintain their good and just lords.'[23]

---

[23] Da Vinci, *Notebooks*, pp. 267–8.

3

RESETTLING IN THE ENGLISH LANGUAGE

The Names of Things

Sunlight in a water bowl on the doorstep
Then on a pond far from home: *soarele*.

Fire in the terracotta hearth, then
In a pit, outside a tent, thousands of miles away: *focul*.

My Black Sea lulling the shore, then dreams
Of sea waking cheeks with stinging salt: *marea*.

Air encircling the grapes outside the window,
Then gliding with a parachute above a heron: *aerul*.

Soil exhaling after rain through gaps between cherry leaves,
Then crying dirty tears from roots of a fallen birch: *pamintul*.[1]

I'd like to explain my relationship with the English language, to offer a glimpse into writing in between languages, histories, and cultures. Though I do not articulate a classification of my national identity in the poetry itself, certain preoccupying questions tend to surface as a matter of belonging to a particular time and place. For instance, do I write as a Romanian, as an American,

---

[1] Carmen Bugan, 'The Names of Things', in *The House of Straw* (Swindon: Shearsman, 2014), p. 46.

Poetry and the Language of Oppression: Essays on Politics and Poetics. Carmen Bugan, Oxford University Press (2021). © Carmen Bugan. DOI: 10.1093/oso/9780198868323.003.0004

a Romanian-American, and how important is it to place my writing in a context that focuses on national identity? In other words, how does one read the poem 'The Names of Things'? The words defined carry the meaning of experiences lived in two places, expressed in a language not accessible to Romanian speakers. English is not the same either; it contains foreign words, memories, and experiences.

While most poets see the loss of their native tongues as akin to death, or at best a condemnation to oblivion, my immigration into the English language presented the possibility to liberate myself from the language of oppression. I say 'liberation' with specific reference to the sense of being able to speak without feeling overheard by hostile listeners. I was leaving behind the language in which I had been humiliated, betrayed, observed, recorded, transcribed, and analyzed by neighbours, relatives, and agents of the State. Years earlier my father concluded 'I don't want to breathe the air for nothing' and stood against injustice. The rather understated vow to silence that my mother had to write and sign before our passports were granted was followed by death threats at the passport office if we talked about what had happened to us. Here is her 'Declaration' in my translation:

Declaration,

The undersigned Mioara Bugan—born Toncu on 5 July 1947 in the village of Draganesti, district of Galati—the daughter of Dumitru and Ortansa, currently living in Draganesti, district of Galati, having received from the State of Romania the approval to leave the country permanently, in order to settle in the United States of America, I assume responsibility never to damage in any way and in any circumstance the interests of the Romanian state and of the Romanian people.

I assume responsibility to remain forever loyal to the Romanian state and to defend its prestige abroad through my activities and through my behaviour.

Signed, Mioara Bugan Date: 25-04-1989

How is a political refugee to defend the interests of a dictatorship abroad, except by complete silence? First, my mother was abused for having remained loyal to her husband; when she was cast out, she was ordered to assume responsibility of loyalty to a state that had literally torn her life apart precisely because her husband defended what he (but not they) regarded as the interests of the Romanian people. By the time she had signed this declaration, my father was accustomed to signing exit briefing forms from prisons, where he undertook not to speak about what he had endured, or about what he had seen other political prisoners endure, on the pain of returning to the chains.

Of course, in the same language I saw the first light of day, experienced the first joys, keened for my dead grandmother, and wrote my first poems. When my family and I arrived in the US, I was 19 years old and all too ready to put the past in its place, to make a clean cut, in the full knowledge that language is not one thing only but many things at the same time. If I was going to live a full life, it was imperative to break free of this language, for I never had an interest in remaining simply a victim. Though I continue to speak Romanian at home, for my writing, I chose to adopt the language of the country in which I had received political asylum, because it had adopted me in its largeness and its largesse: thirty years ago my family and I were welcomed as immigrants, rather than being seen as foreign, polluting influences. The brand-new language, where for me there was no history of political and personal oppression, represented a decisive chance of a kinder future, despite the difficulties ahead. And, yes, I for one wanted to claim the right to tell my story—not to expose the State, not go on trial, but to write myself free, and to write against silence.

Looking back on the past three decades, I see that as a writer I have been searching for the language of freedom—that 'language within language' that depends on particulars of experience with words, and resists the constraints of unreflective conventional usage. It's the language 'inside' the Romanian in which I wrote the family poems when we lived under surveillance; the same one I had to find in English by trial and error. Robert Frost has said that 'poetry is what is lost in translation'[2] but for me poetry is what's irrepressible. The language of my birth is a fundamental part of my poetry in English. Indeed, as a consequence of the births of my children and living in several countries, I have found myself becoming able to return to the language of early childhood, which has remained alive in my memory. This joyful source serves to recall the Romanian experience in the poetry in English in its fullness, acknowledging the experience of both abundance of love and the cruelty of injustice.

The condition of the poet who writes in a non-native language oscillates between self-translation and complete assimilation, and is based on a continuous re-evaluation and re-negotiation of the relationship with the abandoned and the adoptive languages. One needs an actual place in language to plant roots—but that place keeps shifting by necessity. Initially it is a language of exile, where poetry is born at different points of contact between languages as

---

[2] Louis Untermeyer, *Robert Frost: A Backward Look* (Ann Arbor: University of Michigan Library, 1964), p. 18.

they recall memories of life lived in the first language. But, first, the physical experience of exile: in *Paradiso*, Dante expresses his loss by recreating the sensory perception of another's bread and the difficulty of going up and down someone else's stairs. The excerpt, which will be familiar to most of Dante's readers, comes from Canto XVII of *Paradiso*, lines 54–60:[3]

> Tu lascerai ogne cosa diletta
>   più caramente; e questo è quello strale
>   che l'arco de lo essilio pria saetta.
> Tu proverai sì come sa di sale
>   lo pane altrui, e come è duro calle
>   lo scendere e 'l salir per l'altrui scale.

My own translation, based on Charles Singleton's literal rendering and commentary, reads:

> You will leave everything you hold
>   dearest; this is what the bow
>   of exile will shoot first.
> You will taste the salt of another's bread
>   and learn the hardship of your path as
>   you descend and mount another's stairs.

Dante no longer tastes the flavour, no longer senses the texture of the bread: he recognizes only the salt in it, exile having partially crippled his sense of something as ordinary and wholesome. Going up and down the stairs is no longer a way of accessing parts of the house: it only makes him feel the weariness, the hardship. One is defined by the experience of losing the familiar.

---

[3] Dante Alighieri, *The Divine Comedy: Paradiso*, vol. 1 Text, trans. Charles S. Singleton (Princeton, NJ: Princeton University Press, 1975), p. 190.

Acknowledging the Loss

Losing the native language, not hearing it spoken, not having it available to explain oneself in it, not knowing the currency of words and how to calibrate one's use of them, shatter all the carefully constructed protective layers of personal identity. At best, for those fleeing oppression, this can be enabling, working as a pathway to internal freedom and self-definition. At worst, it can be debilitating. The immigrant, the exile, experiences both extremes before settling at the crossroads as a creature with a mind in two places at once. My mind returns again and again to Mowbray's exile speech in *Richard II*, which I read when I had learned enough English to cross over from the Romanian translations of the plays. This was more than a speech: it expressed how I felt as an outcast immigrant to America.

The sense of banishment in the speech, in the Shakespearean world, that implacable 'never to return' helped me form, from a literary perspective, rather than from real-life experience, an understanding of the language of oppression wielded from a place of power. I also discovered a way to explain the feeling of being cast off, in poetry. This in turn showed me that poetry and politics have far more in common than Joseph Brodsky had admitted to himself, when he said that they only share the letters 'p' and 'o'.[4] Poetry can articulate the damage done by political decisions. Here is the speech:

> *Richard II*: The hopeless word of "never to return"
> Breathe I against thee, upon pain of life.

---

[4] Joseph Brodsky, quoted in Lev Loseff, 'Politics/Poetics', in *Brodsky's Poetics and Aesthetics*, ed., Lev Loseff and Valentina Polukhina (Basingstoke: Macmillan, 1990), p. 34.

Thomas Mowbray: A heavy sentence, my most sovereign liege,
And all unlook'd for from your Highness' mouth:
A dearer merit, not so deep a maim
As to be cast forth in the common air,
Have I deserved at your Highness' hands.
The language I have learnt these forty years,
My native English, now I must forgo:
And now my tongue's use is to me no more
Than an unstringed viol or a harp,
Or like a cunning instrument cas'd up,
Or, being open, put into his hands
That knows no touch to tune the harmony:
Within my mouth you have enjail'd my tongue,
Doubly portcullis'd with my teeth and lips,
And dull unfeeling barren ignorance
Is made my jailer to attend on me.
I am too old to fawn upon a nurse,
Too far in years to be a pupil now:
What is thy sentence [then] but speechless death,
Which robs my tongue from breathing native breath?[5]

The use of the word 'or' reveals the mental pressure Mowbray experiences as he reaches for image after image to describe what he foresees it will feel like to cross the border of his country without a language to help make himself understood. Each 'or' opened a space for me in Mowbray's speech, where my memories could unfurl—the packing of the suitcase, the study of English from school books, and a dictionary my father gave us to prepare for the journey ahead, the very English which I dreamed of learning as a child who could never dream of living in another language. To be sure, we had quite possibly escaped death; exile was what had

[5] William Shakespeare, Richard II, Act I, Scene iii, in *The Riverside Shakespeare*, ed., G. Blakemore Evans (Boston: Houghton Mifflin Company, 1974), p. 810.

immediately and decisively saved us. Yet the experience of those first years with no command of English was deeply alienating.

Later on, when we explained in our newly-learned language what had happened to us, we seemed to our hosts less than believable, because our experience in Romania had no equivalent in America. Jailed and tortured for a protest? House arrest? I asked myself if our story was of use to anyone else. Explaining what it was like to be persecuted in one language and free in another, and whether everything was as clear or as simple as that, easily reduced to the dichotomy Romanian = Oppression, English = Freedom left me defensive and frustrated. My understanding of freedom has changed with fluency in the English language: so many are not free in the land we, prospective political refugees from behind the Iron Curtain had imagined full 'of milk and honey'; and the language has strong undercurrents that take time and patience to learn. I confess that unease sets in these days, when the present begins to look like the past and the foundations of my adoptive country are, it seems, being shaken. As I watch statues of American presidents brought down and set on fire during protests against slavery, I am reminded of how volatile and complex we are as communities and how difficult it is—and always has been—to govern ourselves, whatever name we put on the political system of the moment. I am also becoming convinced more than ever of the importance of reaching for the common ground of hope, and the necessity of speaking against bitterness, and against silence, which Milosz has said 'is slavery'.[6]

---

[6] Czeslaw Milosz, 'An Appeal', in *New and Collected Poems: 1931–2001* (London: Allen Lane, 2001), p. 270.

Writing Poetry in English

I began writing in English at what might be called the 'confluence' of languages, nourished by unfamiliar sounds of words, at first translating my poems from memory. Here is an excerpt from an essay published in in 2004, where I was asked to explain why, as a poet, I had relinquished my native language:

> My experience of writing poetry in English can best be explained by telling you about the making of the poem about my parents' divorce. In Romanian, years ago, I called it "Divortul" or "The Divorce". When I began dreaming in English and when the words started to come to me in English, I felt an undercurrent of newness inside. There was freedom and exhilaration: my tongue was slowly getting untied and I wanted to see what it all sounded like in my new language. First I wrote what I remembered of the poem in Romanian and then I tried to translate it: it was called, successively, "The Courtroom," "An Oath of Love," and finally "The Divorce". Many of the first English versions had too many explanations in them: why my mother was forced to divorce, what happened in the courtroom – as though the whole history of the country needed to be told just so that the poetry itself could come through. Then, as I got more settled in my "far away" place, I learned how the narrative could be put into images which conjure back the narratives. And so it happened with many other poems, until the English language began to thrill me with its sounds and the Romanian words never returned to translate the poems back. Lately I think that it would take much effort to put the culture I am writing from now into the Romanian culture I had left just before the Revolution. And if I tried to write in Romanian now, it would be more like going back home on an old (linguistic) map.[7]

---

[7] Carmen Bugan, 'Why I do not write in my native language', *Modern Poetry in Translation*, 3(2), (2004): pp. 7–9.

I will quote from the original poem in Romanian, the first translation of it in English, and then give the poem in its final version in English. The major shift is in the point of view: the 'I' of the poem in the original is the girl speaking directly to her father from the heart of her pain. The woman in the final English version is removed in terms of time, experience, and language; she speaks as an objective narrator, who is able to see the courtroom scene with a certain detachment. I believe that the English language facilitated this necessary change of perspective, which is part of the creative process. Having to relate the experience of a politically determined divorce in the language of a society in which such things do not happen, required letting go of the immediacy of the original, in which I, the speaker of the poem, spoke directly to my father, in the context of a family event: an experience that was essentially not meant for the ears of the public (for I couldn't have read my poem aloud in the house, let alone publish it):

Unde eşti tăticule?
Lacriminile-mi curg şiroaie.
De ce-ai plecat tată?
Ai lăsat in urma furtuni şi ploaie.

Sărută-ne tată,
Sărută-ne pe noi
Că nu se ştie niciodată
Când vom ieşi din noroi.

Daddy, where are you?
My tears flow and flow.
Father, why did you leave us
Inside thunderstorms?

Now kiss us, father,
Bless us with kisses,

For we don't know when
We'll come out of this mud.[8]

By the time I was 15 years old, and had written this poem, I was immersed in the soulful, plangent, and philosophical poetry of Mihai Eminescu (1850–89), who was considered our last Romantic and the first to lay the foundations of Modernism in our national poetry. His language was simple and musical, his thoughts profoundly appealing to my sense of desolation, and though he was taught to us at school as someone who represented nationhood, he created a different world in language from the verse-propaganda practised at the time. I was drawn to his poems of love and nature. He offered an escape, and I had internalized the rhythms and the tone of his poetry. Echoes of two poems by Eminescu can be heard in my original version of 'The Divorce' even through the unsteady handling of language. The first comes from his poem 'Dintre sute de catarge' ['Of the hundreds sailboats'] about the fragility of what's within and the cruelty of what's outside, and how one will never be understood by others. 'Of the hundreds of sailboats'[9] ends:

> Nențeles rămâne gândul
> Ce-ți străbate cânturile,
> Zboară vecinic, îngânându-l,
> Valurile, vânturile.

In my unrhymed translation, this reads:

> No-one understands the thought
> That wanders through your songs,

[8] Carmen Bugan, *Burying the Typewriter* (London: Picador, 2012), p. 143.

[9] Mihai Eminescu, 'Dintre sute de catarge', in *Poezii* (Bucuresti: Biblioteca Pentru Toti, 1960), p. 297.

It flies eternally mocked
By wind, by waves.

A second poem by Eminescu is 'La steaua' ['To the star'],[10] a piece that meditates on the light of the star which reaches our eye long after the star has died. The penultimate stanza:

Icoana stelei ce-a murit
Încet pe cer se suie;
Era pe cînd nu s-a zărit,
Azi o vedem și nu e.

In my translation, again, this reads:

The icon of the star that died
Slowly ascends the sky:
When it lived, it was not seen,
We see it when it's gone.

The sounds of this poetry were in the first pieces I wrote in my youth in a way which was instinctual. My poem, written directly to my father, in the simplest and most direct language I knew, had its roots in the poetry that was nourishing me. For all the silence imposed on me in my native language, I uttered those cries in the cocoon of home. Here again is the first stanza of the poem 'The Divorce' I wrote in Romania in 1985:

Unde ești tăticule?
Lacriminile-mi curg șiroaie.
De ce-ai plecat tată?
Ai lăsat in urma furtuni și ploaie.

---

[10] Mihai Eminescu, 'La Steaua', in *Poezii* (Bucuresti: Biblioteca Pentru Toti, 1960), p. 208.

During the 1990s, I was building a home in a different language, and I would say that the sound and the cadences of Romanian were the most immediate loss. My first English was the English written on food and medicine labels, travelling directions, and textbooks. It took some years to step on the ground of the literary language: that suggestive, deep, rich, and disorientating landscape, where I couldn't sense what was underneath. (In my Romanian, the ground had a cemetery, a buried typewriter, and buried bottles of sunflower oil, all of which eventually have made their way into my poems in English.)

It was the work of the Polish poet Czeslaw Milosz, who had resettled in America decades earlier, writing 'I learned at last to say: this is my home' in a rare poem in English ('To Raja Rao',[11]) that was to remain a source of sustenance for me. His biography is inextricably linked to his writing and I found comfort in his unease. Milosz, who in the same poem characterizes himself as 'Ill at ease in the tyranny, ill at ease in the republic', yearning for freedom in one and the end of corruption in the other, found stability in language: 'To find my home in one sentence, concise, as if hammered in metal' ['To find my home'].[12] This is not to enchant or to earn fame, he says in the same poem, but to resist 'chaos and nothingness', that is, to do something beyond expressing his private sorrows. His devotion to his native language—'my faithful mother tongue'—has never wavered; in the poem with the same name (translated by Milosz and Robert Pinsky) he professes to offer his language 'little bowls of color, bright and pure if

[11] Czeslaw Milosz, 'To Raja Rao', in *New and Collected Poems: 1931–2001* (London: Allen Lane, 2001), p. 254.

[12] Czeslaw Milosz, 'To find my home…', in *New and Collected Poems: 1931–2001*, p. 452.

possible' because, he says, 'perhaps after all it's I who must try to save you'.[13] How this poem unsettled the self I had begun building in my adopted language, and how his poem 'Preface'[14] (translated by Milosz and Robert Hass), where he advises 'First, plain speech in the mother tongue./ Hearing it you should be able to see' searched me! I felt that I had failed a sacred duty to my native language. And I needed to find a way to bring my Romania into the English language.

One must recognize that history happens to one person at a time, and that each one of us has an individual and personal relationship with language. I had to make my own way. In what I am calling self-translation, I needed to carry myself as a human being first into the new language before I could intuit what it was possible to bring in, and what was not, and what sounded off-key. Then, as I achieved fluency, I could take liberties with the original of 'The Divorce' to the point where the original poem echoed through, many years later—even if the original shape and sound had been replaced. The transformation in the new poem may best be described with the images of growing from within and simultaneously stepping outside boundaries that Yves Bonnefoy created in his poem 'L'arbre, la lampe':[15]

> L'arbre vieillit dans l'arbre, c'est l'été.
> L'oiseau franchit le chant de l'oiseau et s'évade.

---

[13] Czeslaw Milosz, 'My faithful mother tongue', in *New and Collected Poems: 1931–2001*, p. 246.

[14] Czeslaw Milosz, 'Preface', in *New and Collected Poems: 1931–2001*, p. 109.

[15] Yves Bonnefoy, 'L'arbre, la lamp', in *New and Selected Poems*, ed., John Naughton and Anthony Rudolf (Chicago: University of Chicago Press, 1995), pp. 74–5.

Emily Grosholz's translation reads:

> The tree grows older in the tree, it's summer.
> The bird traverses birdsong and escapes.

Here is the poem, as published, with one small change, in 2004:

The Divorce

Before they brought him to the courtroom, they gave him
Three apples: 'Your wife sent you these.'
He cradled each apple in the cup of his hands,
The smoothness of their skin became the cheeks of each child.

Inside the courthouse there was a quiet opening and closing of doors.
A crowd of people was chanting his name under the windows.
When the door opened, I saw his bare feet in brown shoes.

His children held each other tight against the wall.
Their breaths, white with cold, were rising towards the ceiling.
They listened for the voices of their parents.

When the divorce was over, he was allowed to see them:
They kissed his chained hands, promised to be good, let their tears fall
On his prison uniform with his own, all three of them burying him.
How I wished we could hide him with our bodies and take him home!

The Securitate peeled us off him.
But we were the apple seeds left to grow
In the sound of his chains on the cement floor.[16]

In writing directly in another language, there is nothing to translate. In the divorce poem—in the English language, and to the English language—I brought the language of poetry up against the

---

[16] Carmen Bugan, 'The Divorce', in *Crossing the Carpathians* (Manchester: Oxford Poets/Carcanet, 2004), p. 17.

language of oppression with an image that expresses the necessity for imagination, as one reaches for self-liberation. The apples—the fruit of childhood, from our own garden, but also the ones the interrogators gave to my father, pretending Mother sent them to make him feel that through divorce he would lose his three children—bear the taste of freedom: even if that figures as seeds on the cement floor. Whether this poem—and all the others—make it possible to identify myself as a Romanian or an American poet, I am not sure myself. I suspect that writing in a non-native language places one in the world family, where national classification seems less urgent than the concern with the themes in poetry that cross boundaries of countries and languages. 'Tu sais que c'est l'obscur de ton cœur qui guérit' [You know, it is the darkness of your heart healing] ends Bonnefoy's poem. *Je sais.*

The Many Houses of Language

Over the past thirty years the English language has become a place where I record the happenings of life and in which I remember the rituals of my childhood. *Grijrea* is still practised around the villages in my part of the country. The ritual says that we must give to others in this life whatever it is that we want to have in the afterlife with us. Its immediate social objective is to give alms to the poor, but its spiritual aim is to bring comfort to the process of dying, to make the afterlife feel familiar. My collection *The House of Straw* is an enactment of this ritual in words. The title poem, below, is a description of the *grijirea* as I witnessed my grandparents perform it. The poem encourages an acceptance of death, but also expresses a deep attachment to life. When I wrote *The House of Straw*, I set out to portray exile as a linguistic afterlife by using this ancient Romanian Orthodox ritual of preparation for the great crossing of the soul. I set out to express the sense of living one life by means of the symbols of the other. Here are the first and the final stanzas of the poem:

'In this world the house will be yours
But in the afterlife it shall be mine.'
So, when they were old, they joined
In the ritual of caring for the band
Of gypsies coming through the village,
Looking after parents left by children
At empty hearths. What you give away
Stays with you in eternity,
For heaven or hell will be received
In a familiar bed, at a table you know.
…

When the poor in this life were called
To receive the roofless houses of straw,
Candles were lit to link living day
To other world with the cord of light;
I watched all those hands uniting
On stems of wax held at thresholds,
I saw love eternal, burning at open doors.
Then in his room, my grandfather brought
A flask of wine, set it on the table, and cried.[17]

In 'The House Founded on Elsewhere',[18] I acknowledge the insufficiency of one language alone to portray the condition of writing in a non-native language, even as I take issue with Emil Cioran's views on the matter in the epigraph to the poem. The final

---

[17] Carmen Bugan, 'The House of Straw', in *The House of Straw* (Swindon: Shearsman, 2014), p. 15.

[18] Carmen Bugan, 'The house founded on elsewhere', in *Releasing the Porcelain Birds* (Swindon: Shearsman, 2016), p. 53.

section, below, voices the acceptance that sometimes we must begin the healing in another language and make the house as strong as we can with the materials we have, understanding perhaps that poetry can be a synthesis of languages.

The House Founded on Elsewhere

He who turns against his language, adopting that of others, changes his identity and even his deceptions. He tears himself—a heroic betrayal—from his own memories, and up to a point, from himself.

(Emil Cioran, from The Temptation to Exist, translated from Romanian by Carmen Bugan)

VII.

Not all the words you say are the Self and not all turning
Against your language is self-betrayal. Behind each word
Is what tries to get inside it. That is what matters

Whether I speak it in my own language
Or in the tongue of others. The thought, the breath
With which you send love out, or forgiveness, say,

Outlive the words and languages, outstrip
The syllables at prayer or play. I speak of smiles and tears
And better yet, smiles through tears at the end of day.

And so the house stands with what it can:
A sagging wall, a brand new door through which
Come children with schoolbooks and road-side flowers;

Solid enough to face the winter wind and baking heat,
Each word inside for what it's worth and what it can say:
Good enough to bear the weight of what's to come.

So, here too, I give in to my own 'temptation to exist'—in English. The poetry is to be found in the leap the heart takes as the mind crosses back and forth between the language of memory, Romanian, and the language of the present, English. To the English language and its poetry, I bring a personal testimony about tyranny. The insertion of the secret police surveillance documents on my family in the poems arising from surveillance performs the function of bringing the language of oppression in direct confrontation with the 'language within language' of poetry, in order to create a sense of resistance. Instead of returning to the language of oppression and dwelling on it (through memory), I carry it to a place where I can put it in a new perspective, expose it, and resist it more effectively. I also bring a nostalgia for a lost world, without the politics in it, as an indication of attachment to certain aspects of the past, maybe those that return to a 'time out of time'.

There is a marvellous poem by the Italian poet Giacomo Leopardi (1798–1837) called 'Il sabato del villaggio' [Saturday in the village],[19] about peasants who spend their Saturday preparing, daydreaming, and anticipating the coming of Sunday: to me, it induces that deeply pleasurable perception of timelessness in the most ordinary and intimate moments of our lives. A girl walks home in the evening from the fields with a sheaf of hay in her arms; in her hands she carries a bouquet of roses and violets which she plans to wear on Sunday. Saturday is the best day, the poem goes on to say, because everyone in the village dreams of the holiday, it's the only day when the worries about daily life are put away. Sunday never seems to arrive. Children play noisily in the square. The older women reminisce about their youthful days when they danced with the handsome men of the village. The cobbler and

---

[19] Giacomo Leopardi, 'Il sabato del villaggio', in *Canti: Giacomo Leopardi*, trans. Jonathan Galassi (New York: Farrar, Straus and Giroux, 2012), pp. 208–211.

the carpenter work after everyone else goes to sleep, anxious to finish before the sunrise, so they too can enjoy the Sunday. It's a poem that recreates a known but lost world, a sense of eternity. But Sunday, the speaker says (and we know), will already bring Monday to mind: the worries, the work, the monotony of the week. The final two lines, where the speaker addresses a playful, mischievous boy, in the bloom of his life, end with a blessing:

> Altro dirti non vo'; ma la tua festa
> Ch'anco tardi a venir non ti sia grave.

Jonathan Galassi, in the bilingual edition *Canti: Giacomo Leopardi*, has translated these lines as:

> I won't say more, but may your Sunday
> That is so slow to come not disappoint you.

In other words, the poem says, may the summer of your life for which you keep preparing and waiting for, be as rich as your imaginings. I have heard that sentiment countless times as a child sitting on the stone steps with my grandparents. Doors to strange, unknown worlds have opened for me, or I have opened them as I wandered through other languages. At times I was surprised to find myself opening a door to a familiar but more distant past too—in the poems in translation—which feels oddly comfortable because it operates at the boundaries between languages, where one sees poetry hard at work trying to break through. Thus, other languages and experiences flow into the English of the present that I am using, bringing news of lives from other places.

Poetry at the Crossroads

Regardless of the particular circumstances by which one arrives at the confluence of languages, T.S. Eliot's contention that 'The serious writer of verse must be prepared to cross himself with the best verse of other languages and the best prose of all languages'[20] is sound advice. In order to belong to the world, one must know it, and to know it, one must travel unfamiliar roads, where surprises, detours, and challenges to one's views on language will emerge in a larger context. Writing in another language takes Eliot's metaphor of 'crossing' to another level, and in this final section I would like to examine the position of the non-native in the English language by looking at the work of the Hungarian poet George Szirtes (1948–), who brings to English a powerful historical testimony written in a language that has travelled through time and countries: a language fully conscious of itself.[21]

Szirtes sees himself as part of the larger world community and likens his poetry to a palimpsest. He and I come from the same corner of Europe and his work feels familiar in the experiences that it brings to life. In an article entitled 'Translation—and migration—is the lifeblood of culture', Szirtes explains something that is obvious to those who read deeply, but contentious to those obsessed with boundaries. One cannot read literature simply in one national

[20] T.S. Eliot, *The Complete Prose of T. S. Eliot*, ed., Ronald Schuchard, 8 vols (London: Project Muse, 2014–) vol. I, p. 679.

[21] The following discussion of Szirtes's work has appeared in an earlier format as two reviews: One is a review of the *New and Collected Poems* (Bloodaxe Books, 2008), published on 21 June 2013 in *Harvard Review* Online: https://www.harvardreview.org/book-review/new-collected-poems/. The other is a review of *The Photographer at Sixteen* (Maclehose Press, 2019), published in *The Manhattan Review*, https://themanhattanreview.com/reviews/photographer-at-sixteen.

context, he says, we must be aware of the international aspect of any major work: 'This form of internationalism is the lifeblood of art. It is rootless, it is cosmopolitan, and it is free thinking.'[22] Unlike me, Szirtes writes both in Hungarian and English and is an avid translator; he can easily be claimed by the English and by the Hungarians as their own. Szirtes has earned international critical praise for a poetry that listens, keens, celebrates, memorializes, and uplifts as it bears testimony to Europe's recent turbulent past. (He has won the T.S. Eliot Prize among many others for his poems and he received a Man Booker International Prize for his translations.)

The repercussions of exile can be traced throughout Szirtes's poetry: from the early decision to address his father with the casual 'You' to the moving series of sonnets 'Portrait of My Father in an English Landscape' and the memory of himself and his father in Budapest in 'Eclogue: Fair Day' where their lives, caught in one instant, seem to blend in the broader picture 'In the way you slip a bus-ticket into a book' which is 'sure to fall out'.[23] What falls out of history, and is, despite everything, retrieved, is a primordial moment now folded, inside the poem, into the larger story of our common past. The condition of being exiles means that father and son will never grow old together walking in Budapest, but somehow the young father and son will be brought back as memories in English without becoming abstract, the way memories do.

---

[22] George Szirtes, 'Translation—and migration—is the lifeblood of culture', *The Guardian*, 6 February 2017, https://www.theguardian.com/books/booksblog/2017/feb/06/translation-and-migration-lifeblood-culture-george-szirtes.

[23] George Szirtes, 'Eclogue: Fair Day', in *New and Collected Poems* (Northumberland: Bloodaxe Books, 2008), p. 401.

In his memoir, *Speak, Memory*, Vladimir Nabokov evokes in lyrical English a childhood sleigh ride remembered while walking in a snowy forest in Vermont:

> The vibration in my ear is no longer their receding bells, but only my old blood singing. All is still, spellbound, enthralled by the moon, fancy's rear-vision mirror. The snow is real, though, and as I bend to it and scoop up a handful, sixty years crumble to glittering frost-dust between my fingers.[24]

Suddenly the Vermont snow has something Russian in it, just as American literature now contains Nabokov's unique language. Much of Szirtes's poetry has a similar effect. It is also the 'old blood singing' from the first collections that experiment with form and expose the clutter of life, to the books from *Portrait of My Father in an English Landscape* onwards that weave music, image, and memory into complex and pellucid verse.

To Szirtes, language becomes, figuratively, the human body. In 'Book', the printed text is 'open like a pair of lungs / Breathing words', and stories, like us, become 'exhausted'.[25] Here we have a comforting vision of the world, where graves are really only bedrooms in the hill, where stories are being spun and spun again, and where the living and the dead coexist, for better or for worse. Here is the old blood singing—in poetry. In his memoir, *The Photographer at Sixteen*, Szirtes brings his mother back to life in a portrait which makes it possible to perceive the face of the turbulent history of Budapest.

---

[24] Vladimir Nabokov, *Speak, Memory* (New York: Everyman's Library, 1999), p. 74.
[25] George Szirtes, 'Book', in *New and Collected Poems* (Northumberland: Bloodaxe Books, 2008), p. 400.

The Hungarian Revolution broke out on 23 October 1956, a Tuesday. By Thursday, the gunfire got closer to a flat in Budapest where two school boys were recovering from scarlet fever, their mother tending to them while waiting for her husband who was late from work. A bullet crashed through the window, hit the ceiling, and landed on the toy watch one of the boys was wearing. This is how the poet, the boy with the toy watch, remembers the Uprising. Communism is one of the historical nightmares that menaced Szirtes's family, who escaped Hungary along with many others who either feared persecution or could no longer find stability in their own country. When he arrived in England as an 8-year-old-boy, the poet remembers wearing only one shoe: the family left in such a rush, and the journey was so harrowing, no one noticed he had forgotten to put on the other shoe. A few days earlier he had walked on the unfolded map of Hungary and its neighbouring countries, spread on the floor of the family home, as if rehearsing. 'One only had to walk, after all',[26] he recalls as he recounts looking at the map with his parents.

Earlier, the Holocaust had taken its toll on both sides of his family. This was true in Cluj, Romania, named in three languages each time it is mentioned—'Cluj or Kolozsvar, also known as Klausenburg'—each language representing a different and painful relationship to the place. But it would also become true later in England, where László and Magda, his parents, gained an apparently safe existence, enjoying job security, buying their first television, a car, and an apartment, putting their children through school, and even managing to have family vacations. There,

---

[26] George Szirtes, *The Photographer at Sixteen* (London: Maclehose Press, 2019), p. 81.

Magda received medical care for her heart condition brought on by rheumatic fever in childhood and exacerbated by a tumultuous life in which she fought and worked for the future of her children. But there, too, Magda, a survivor of two labour camps and a woman whose dreams were repeatedly shattered, ended her own life.

In *The Photographer at Sixteen*, Szirtes looks for evidence of hope, for memories, and for a coherent story in countries, languages, and places that feel like half-opened doors, allowing only glimpses into his mother's life. She was a photographer and, according to him, the best photographs she took were of her children. But at times she would fly into a rage and would scratch out the faces of her children, or her own face, from the photographs. He writes, 'The sheer fury of her effacement was shocking.' He connects his mother's violence towards the photographs with the violence of history, which renders people unrecognizable: 'We work our way back through history through a forest of wiped faces...Bones in mass graves.'[27] History in Szirtes's narrative is particular and personal, the emerging details giving us an understanding of the losses his family endured in order to survive. Cluj is a place where the Hungarian people were forbidden by the Romanian communist government to speak their language and Szirtes remembers the oppressive atmosphere of the city during a visit to see his mother's family. On that occasion, his uncle remained silent on the taxi ride home from the train station, out of fear of being arrested and jailed if he spoke Hungarian. He writes about how this hostility towards the Hungarian Jews affected his mother's sense of belonging to place, language, and people.

[27] Ibid., p. 44.

The language of Szirtes's memoir brings place and detail, faces, and cityscapes to life, recovers, and puts them before the reader. At the train station in Cluj, the lady at the ticket office advises passengers seeking information about schedules to 'Come down when your train is due and see whether it comes or not.'[28] Buda and Pest are separate in their respective opulence and despondence, and disparate events in both parts of the city begin falling into place like pieces of a puzzle. The family names change to cover up their Jewish roots, and Szirtes remarks, 'The clutter and confusion of names is like a constant noise in the head.'[29] This effort to reconstruct the past, to understand it, is a direct confrontation with oblivion.

Szirtes finds photographs and he looks at them with the eye of an archivist, a poet, an artist, and a son who yearns for his mother and searches for her so far back in time, he reaches her tender childhood. He looks at and describes family photographs, but then he goes further: in one of the most beautiful and profound passages in the book, he meditates on a photograph of his mother as a child:

> But her childhood gaze goes beyond vulnerability. There is, I am beginning to think, something mystical about it, as if she were rapt by a vision, a miracle beyond the conjurer's art. Maybe she has been vouchsafed a vision of her own incomprehensible future. I know the photographs are still, but time tumbles about them chaotically, future and past indistinguishable, simultaneous, like voices in a storm. The storm seems to freeze for a moment but will not settle and starts up again.[30]

---

[28] Ibid., p. 162.
[29] Ibid., p. 111.
[30] Ibid., p. 195.

Of course, Szirtes gazes into these pictures from the future (his present), with the knowledge of what will become of her, as he himself tumbles through time and tries to make sense of her suicide. She will never know how he searches for her. He realizes painfully that he could not have been truly available to her in his early childhood even though she often told him that he was a comfort for her, and he regrets being away from her when he was older. He admits he often imagines her and in movingly direct language, he says:

> I want to report her presence and register it as it moved through life by moving back into her own past with her. I want to puzzle over it and admire it while being aghast at it. I don't want to be certain of anything. I don't want to come to conclusions.[31]

In broader terms, this book offers a clear understanding of how historical upheaval tears through the individual's relationship with life itself. Szirtes traces his mother's lack of trust in people to the neighbours turning against each other, first during the mass deportation of Jewish people, then on the return home of the survivors, and later yet during the communist horror when everyone was either an informer or the one informed on, where some were being hanged from the lampposts of Budapest while others were running through muddy woods to what they imagined would be freedom. It is a catalogue of human deception and yet his mother showed a heroic will to survive it all, and even thrive. At one point his mother becomes Budapest itself:

> I am reading this into her. The bullet holes and shell marks on Budapest buildings were her wounds. The blasted statuary that

---

[31] Ibid., p. 71.

projected from wall after wall was her. She was a piece of broken statuary. I understood this process as I understood her, in other words, hardly at all.[32]

The narrative brings us face to face with the consequences of political decisions that are beyond the power or even the comprehension of an individual, and yet somehow they become part of the collective burden. The violence on the streets enters violently within us. Generations are left grieving and searching for answers. And yet there are no hard feelings, no self-righteousness, no preaching coming from Szirtes; just the sense that the poet is 'aghast' at the inescapable history. Bullet holes and marks as wounds, mother as broken statuary. In another place Magda is imagined as a speaker in a poem, young, on the train to the labour camp:

> They put me on a train, east, west, or south
> As we rode off in different directions,
> Myself, my body and my heart. My eyes
> Were saying something to my open mouth
> Which had remained open in surprise,[33]

The poem makes it possible for the mother to speak through the words of her son, for the painful history of one country to rise in the language of another: this is a remarkable victory over silence and oblivion. If the violence of history can undermine our will to live, there is still the possibility of measured, generous, and gentle words that, although unable to forestall violence, can still bear witness to it. The beautiful English in this memoir, written by a

---

[32] Ibid., p. 148.
[33] Ibid., p. 125.

Hungarian refugee, has the piercing power of a child's call for his absent mother: a call we can all hear.

Conclusion: Breaking the Silence in Another Language

Truth is like water: when it comes across the rocks of silence and fear, it flows around them, over and under, carving the river bed as it courses from one language into another. It takes a long time for the water to weaken the rocks and turn them into sand. Oppression is as durable as freedom. We are too far along into the human story to go all the way to the beginning to understand how it all started, so for many of us the healing may just have to come from the journey that we begin mid-way, in other languages. Eventually the news will return to the source, but it will not change the past: we are the ones who will change. My experience of communist oppression is a small instance of oppression in history, yet the need for freedom—personal, artistic, existential—is translatable across continents, times, and languages. Some things are useful to carry from one language into another: the aromas of food, old healing rituals, family, and (for me) some words too: *marea, aerul, pamintul, soarele, focul.* We have the language of poetry, the language of literature—that 'language within language'—to help us carry the burdens of our lives, in the same way water moves the rocks slowly downstream, towards the sea.

As for a definition of freedom, there is a passage from Laurie Lee's memoir *As I Walked Out One Midsummer Morning,* which speaks very well to the sense of leaving everything familiar behind, not because one is forced to do so, but because one chooses. In expressing the feeling of being almost oppressed by freedom the day he left his home to explore the world, Lee has spoken also for my own experience of leaving my native language to make my own discoveries:

> I was free. I was affronted by freedom. The day's silence said, Go where you will. It's all yours. You asked for it. It's up to you now. You're on your own, and nobody's going to stop you. As I walked, I was taunted by echoes of home, by the tinkling sounds of the kitchen, shafts of sun from the windows falling across the familiar furniture, across the bedroom and the bed I had left.[34]

---

[34] Laurie Lee, *As I Walked Out One Midsummer Morning* (Boston: David R. Godine, 2011), p. 3.

4

ARTISTIC DISTANCE AND THE LANGUAGE OF OPPRESSION

For me, the most difficult aspect of writing about pain, whether personal or public, is the fear that the expression of suffering courts, gratuitously, the sympathy of the reader. The other difficulty arises in re-experiencing the pain, because it brings to the surface other emotions, anger among them. Writers take these risks frequently, either because they have been victims of oppression, or because they feel the urgency to revolt against the status quo. The unfortunate result is that writing appears to be *about* being a victim, or becomes vengeful polemic, or else turns into language aiming to 'shock the reader' into the 'realization' of others' suffering, or into 'consciousness' of various forms of injustice.[1] It's

---

[1] See, for example, Catrin Gersdorf's discussion of writers raising environmental awareness by conflating 'pure aesthetics with volatile moral issues' and by using the emotions of 'fear, disorientation and surprise' which will 'shock the readers into a heightened consciousness', in Catrin Gersdorf, *The Poetics and Politics of the Desert: Landscape and the Construction of America* (Amsterdam: Rodopi, 2009), p. 203. Compare this approach with Sigurd F. Olson's sublime writing on nature, as part of his work as an activist, in Sigurd F. Olson, *The Singing Wilderness* (Minneapolis: University of Minnesota Press, 1997; reprinted, 1945 first edition). See also, the essay by Robert Combs, 'The Eternal Now in *Brave New World*: Huxley, Joseph Campbell, and *The Perennial Philosophy*', in *Huxley's Brave New World: Essays*, ed. David Garrett Izzo and Kim Kirkpatrick (Jefferson, NC: McFarland and Co., 2014). p. 161. The technique is well known, but it only represents one way of relating to language.

Poetry and the Language of Oppression: Essays on Politics and Poetics. Carmen Bugan, Oxford University Press (2021). © Carmen Bugan. DOI: 10.1093/oso/9780198868323.003.0005

a double exposure: the vulnerability of an admission of feeling hurt and uneasy in the world, and the risk of opening complex emotional, intellectual, and creative spaces where somehow the reader feels imposed upon. It threatens the principle of writing as an offering. Writing a personal story when it is a part of other people's stories—and concerns public duress—compounds these difficulties. Equanimity is not necessarily a natural state: it is acquired through trial and error, and the process of writing itself has a crucial role in helping to achieve and maintain it, but not unless the phenomenon of being moved by and moving (*movere*) by literary language is clearly understood.

In order to extend the capacities of lyric expression as it incorporates the language and experience of oppression (coming from outside agents) and the suppressive language (which is in part a form of self-protection, and in part a retreat inwards as acceptance that changes cannot take place in one's situation), the writer must walk the line between passion and tranquillity. Lyric language succeeds if the feelings conveyed resonate, or find an echo in the emotional context of society: with this comes a sense of liberation, because the writer is 'heard', and feeling heard generates a sense of validation that something has been communicated successfully. This is not the same as seeking to offer consolation by denying the misfortunes that afflict people's lives or their societies: to minimize the hurt, as Miguel de Unamuno affirms in his book, *The Tragic Sense of Life*, 'is another misfortune in addition'.[2] And it is not the same as encouraging an acceptance of hopelessness

[2] Miguel de Unamuno, *The Tragic Sense of Life*, trans. J.E. Crawford Flitch (New York: Dover Publications, 1954), p. 304. (Unamuno quotes Calderon, as he rightly makes the case against focusing solely on the 'immeasurable beauty of life' and persuading people that 'the misfortunes' people suffer 'are not misfortunes'.)

either. So, the question that arises beforehand is this: 'How does language determine how I wish to be understood and not be misunderstood?'

To my mind, the aim of literature is not to transform pain into art in order to glorify suffering for its own sake, despite the common beliefs that pain and suffering ennoble the soul, forge the character, and provide artistic inspiration. We venerate heroes for the higher values they represent. Their suffering—their sacrifice—indicates the deep, inevitable conflicts in societies over values, politics, economic realities, and so on. We take inspiration from the way in which people maintain their values despite the pain inflicted on them, and we deeply admire those who take control over their anguish and overcome it. Beyond this, suffering is unpleasant, dull, and uninteresting in and of itself and most of us are keen to avoid it. Literature, and poetry, recreate and revisit pain in order to talk about its sources and its implications, as well as to mark the existence of our lives and the lives of others.

The transformation occurs in *us*—readers—because we recognize ourselves or aspects of our situation in others, so that when we feel someone else's hardship, we share a common bond. 'Recognition (*anagnorisis*)', said Aristotle, 'is a change from ignorance to knowledge of a bond of love or hate between persons', which, in return, will 'evoke pity or fear'.[3] The writer trusts and counts on bringing about that 'change from ignorance to knowledge' in the reader, to facilitate an identification of the reader with the speaker or the situation evoked. 'Tragedy', said Aristotle, achieves 'the purgation (catharsis)' of 'pity and fear' by creating

---

[3] Aristotle, *On Poetry and Style*, trans. G.M.A. Grube (Indianapolis: Hackett, 1958), pp. 21–2.

them for the reader, who contemplates them.[4] In other words, literature helps us to gain perspective, or to overcome suffering, rather than sublimate it into art. As writers who feel the emotions we are portraying, we often have to position ourselves in relation to them, rather than allowing ourselves to be swallowed by them; we must locate the right approach to the language of oppression rather than allowing ourselves to be overwhelmed by it. The balance rests, I think, in finding the means to merge the private (I suffer) and the public (the world suffers just as much) into a unifying voice that can communicate the emotions the writer feels and wants to convey, for the benefit of others. But, first, I shall consider the sense of being moved by writing and by reading works of literature.

Dante expressed the process of recognition, and also the feeling of being moved, at the end of *Paradiso*, in terms which clarify the effects of writing I aim to articulate in this chapter. At the end of his journey, the poet reaches the 'Living Light', which he calls also the 'Light Eternal'. As he gazes upon it, his eyesight becomes clearer, stronger, fortified, his vision strengthened by looking. This expresses the union of the self with the divine, as the divine, which holds everyone in its light, imparts itself to the individual; Canto XXXIII, line 132: 'per che 'l mio viso in lei tutto era messo': 'my whole face was placed inside the light'.[5] The face of the poet is mirrored, recognizes itself, in the eternal light of being. This could be read as a metaphor that expresses the union of the writer with language, for one feels understood and reflected in language, and language is comprehensible because the individual is a part of it. The image of light Dante sees becomes clearer while he looks

[4] Ibid., p. 12.
[5] Dante Alighieri, *The Divine Comedy: Paradiso*, 1, Text, trans. Charles S. Singleton (Princeton, NJ: Princeton University Press, 1975), p. 378.

upon it, because it has entered him. As Dante is changed by looking at the divine light, and sees his own face in it, so the writer is transformed by the process of writing, which is essentially an act of searching deeply into language for illumination. The stanza below voices this recognition of being moved—starting from one place and finding oneself changed (Canto XXXIII, lines 112–14):[6]

> ma per la vista che s'avvalorava
>   in me guardando, una sola parvenza,
>   mutandom' io, a me si travagliava.

In my translation, based on Charles Singleton's translation and commentary, this reads:

> my sight became clearer as I looked
>   into the light that appeared to me as one,
>   and worked itself inside me, as I was changing.

I proceed from the idea of writing as a process that effects inner change, and by extension reading as a transformative process, in the precise sense articulated by Dante: transformation of one's vision from blurriness to clarity, which makes it possible to see the object of contemplation become clearer as one focuses on it. This view of language allows me to convey the sense of oppression factually, emotionally, intellectually, and more importantly to begin the journey of writing towards healing and freedom without creating a burden of emotion on the reader. It takes writing closer to Aristotle's injunction 'to realize a greater good or avoid a greater evil' in 'The Representation of Evil'.[7] Begging the sympathy

---

[6] Ibid., p. 378.
[7] Aristotle, *On Poetry and Style*, p. 56.

of the reader, writing from a sense of self-pity, sermonizing, or writing in such a way as to arouse more anger and revenge, represent the great failures of art, as much as painting a false veneer of optimism on a tragic situation, or avoiding reality all together because somehow it does not conform to a definition of appropriate 'artistic material'.

But then, what happens next? Even more important is being able to grasp the process that takes place after everyone—writer and reader alike—absorbs the precise sense of oppression or injustice. That question of 'what next?' is just as important as the question of 'why write?'. The writer's challenge is to understand the processes of language that lead to oppressive conditions and to use that understanding as a healing resource that contributes to overcoming injustice. I believe we must try to understand the nature of suffering, the mechanism by which pain challenges us, but we can only achieve this if the story is about language, not simply about the writer. If the story is only about the writer or about one historical moment, the work will cease to be of interest beyond the life of the author or the news cycle—which unfortunately is the case with much of the current literature that refers only to one's own experience, or depends on 'topical' imagery. But if the poem shows *how language works* in the life of the individual, in a moment of history, then the rewards are bountiful: first, the writer heals his or her own pain through the catharsis that takes place through revisiting and recreating the pain; second, the work becomes a catalyst for public catharsis, because it offers a clear and true linguistic perspective on suffering. The knowledge about how language works translates into a view of language as an ally, where words become effective tools of resistance. So how do we write, insightfully, 'above' our condition?

My writing explores the subject of the actual lived life. Since my own life has been shaped by forces of history—political oppression and exile—the language which forms the larger part of my material is the language of oppression, the language which suppresses and reduces the individual, making life disorderly and unpredictable. So the more capacious question of how to sublimate language into art takes on particular nuances. How do we face loss with language? What happens when language is stolen from us? Can the lyric language which I create be coherent if I am emotionally incoherent myself? What happens to the authorial voice when personal biography fuses with the lyric 'I'? What are the effects of writing on well-being?

'A Birthday Letter': Censorship and the Language of Family

In 2013, I returned to Romania with my family, using the secret police maps that document my father's movements around the country, and the maps of our memory. Together, we visited the prisons where my father had been tortured for twelve years during the communist repression. He was incarcerated in the 1960s and then again in the 1980s and I wanted to see what was on the other side of the visiting room doors, especially in the Aiud prison, a place which had marked my sense of identity as a daughter of a political criminal. I also wanted to see the Iron Curtain through my father's eyes: the story of his escape all the way to the border with Turkey, through Bulgaria, had formed a part of my mental furniture for many years, as I listened to him. We flew separately from different countries, met in Bucharest, and went on a car journey of over 2,000 km.

I wanted to write about this experience. I returned to Romania both as a member of my family and as the storyteller of my family, a writer; the full realization of that role gave me a path into pain which I would not have opened up, had I gone without the intention of writing. What could have simply been a trip to understand us, as a family, developed into a journey in search of the words that would have to carry the weight of actual events and a clear articulation of poetics. As a writer, I was in search of poetic language. As my parents' child, I was given privileged access into their past before I existed, wandering thus into places that were unsynchronized with the normal rhythms of life. They entrusted to me a task—to understand and tell their story, to talk about their memories and memory gaps, so that together we could correct the record, and reclaim our own words from a narrative which was not written by us, but had so many of our words in it.

I shall pause on two moments from that trip, in order to reflect on approaching suffering in the language of poetry. How is one to tap into the significance of memories? The first moment is about finding missing prison letters (those we sent to each other and have 'received' some thirty years later). This discovery led me to reflect on the power of the State to confiscate private moments from people, stealing the language that sustains them. The loss I experienced in reading the files was a loss of language, as I was reading a different Romanian of betrayal from the one I had known, and a different Romanian from the beautiful village language I had learned as a child and that had sustained me throughout my life, as a source of innocence and happiness. Most of the recovered correspondence between my father and us was transcribed and paraphrased, and so it contained the transcriber, as a third 'presence' in our lives, and a third 'factor' in language. Below are two short letters from the family archives that show how our correspondence was censored (we had written them in the 1980s). I include also a note from an informer documenting my mother's distress that our packages were not getting through to my father in prison.

TV/S/00973 from 9.XI.1985
Nr. ex. 2, ex. 1 at I.M.I.
NOTE

The source informs you that Bugan Ioan from Aiud Str. Morii 7-9 told his daughter Bugan Carmen from the commune of Draganesti that he is waiting for news from home or to be called at a prison visit but it is all in vain. He asks her what is happening with her mommy, if she is ill or angry. He received his package with food and medication.

He has a right to a prison visit and they could go when they want, they can go on the 5th.

He asks Mioara to send him a package. He thanks them and awaits news from home.

18.02.1986
Major Plt. Florea
Mj. Gelu
Note of Information 014/009282

The source informs you that on the day of 16-02-1986 he met Mioara Bugan from the commune of Draganesti. The source asked her how and what she is doing these days and she said that she is worried about her husband Bugan Ion to whom she is sending packages and who doesn't receive them. She doesn't know why this is. She also said that since she divorced him she lost her right to visit him. She now works at the Cooperative Earnest. I inform you that this woman is now only visited by (*and here the text is all covered in black ink*).

Signature (illegible)
18.02.1986
Bugan Mioara is being followed with the type of D.U.I. and is monitored for information.

TV/S/00997 from 23 October 1986
Nr ex 2 ex 1 at 1.B.I.
(unintelligible note)
NOTE

The source informs you that Bugan Ioan at Aiud, Str. Morii 7-9 Alba district, told Mioara Bugan from the commune of Draganesti that he received the package with the medicines and thanks them, but he did not receive a letter from them with news following the earthquake. He is asking his wife to clarify about Carmen, how many years she will have to study at the agriculture high school and at which level she entered the high school, seeing that she had already studied for 10 years. He asks for prescription glasses +2, ulcer medication, garlic, onion, and lard. In December he hopes they will send him another package with food. He salutes them with sentiments of esteem and respect.

Reading these letters, decades after they had been written, and imagining their journey from our hands through different secret police desks, files, and boxes, I wondered how many other people are still reading their own censored letters and how they feel about something as amorphous as 'the State' meddling in the private life of a family. I wondered about the role of surveillance and censorship and how they affect our sense of safety. I thought about censorship in relation to the power of language, and whether it is an intrinsic part of the language of power. And of course, I was heartbroken, and felt as if I was somehow opening old wounds. Walking through the village with my family on that visit, the words of the letters making a sort of white noise in my mind, was a slightly defamiliarizing experience: though we knew we had been observed all those years back, having the secret police transcripts alive in my mind as I was looking at people made me feel as if I was looking *through* them.

The poem, 'A Birthday Letter' takes its cue from one letter we did receive from my father, on his 50th birthday, in which he had asked us to make a cake for him. But the poem is not meant to indict, or to testify against the secret police, or to function as anti-communist propaganda. The aim was to write myself out of pain, using the language of poetry, while bringing to life a moment that shows the uses and abuses of language. As a poet, I was looking for lessons that could be learned from this material—about language. One of these lessons has to do with how the oppressor disorients the victim by suppressing communication and intimidating the victim into silence. Lyric language gave me a means to do something useful about dealing with a traumatic past, so what began as a process of thinking about actual events, and their significance, turned into a process of thinking about the appropriate language through which I could put 'feeling into words' to use Seamus Heaney's expression about his own work, in which words were seen as bearers of history, rather than simply private lyric utterance.[8] I have reached for images in the larger literature: the myth of Apollo and Marsyas, a metaphor which I thought worked well to express the sense of having language stripped away from me. It became important to use figurative language not as ornament but to make it absolutely essential in conveying the meaning of the experience, so that I could portray certain realities and express feelings according to my own independent viewpoint.

At the heart of this was my belief that history—and oppression—happen in the minutiae of our lives, and that poetry can make them both emotionally intelligible. I enjoyed the long moments of concentration when the mind was focused on line length, on the sound of words, on creating the simile of words as capillaries. Keeping the

---

[8] Seamus Heaney, 'Feeling into words', in *Preoccupations* (New York: Farrar, Straus and Giroux, 1981), pp. 41–60.

mind occupied with composing the poem gave me a respite from the anger I felt at what had been done to us; it felt good to see more clearly into the experience and put a shape to it. Here is the poem:

A birthday letter

The words 'the source informs you' echo in my head
that *other* voice—familiar, comfortable almost,

lining our private cries: 'the inmate wrote'
to his wife and children 'from the Aiud prison'.

Our letters journeyed through the clay-like
maze of secret police desks. Stamps, checks, dates,

signatures indicate officers and places. The paraphrase
of ongoing pain—half the time they paraphrased us.

That voice in introductions sticks to our words
like a skin disease impossible to cure. But then

some sentences from us burst free perhaps because
they're not translatable, editable, condensable.

They stand out in quotation marks:
unexpected missing heartbeats.

On 4 May 1985 my father thought about his birthday:
'Make a cake with fifty candles and take a picture.'

I recall the cake on our kitchen table,
and thinking about him in chains that day.

'My dear, the children are healthy', Mother said.
'Come to see me with my children', he said.

'Do you remember me coming home with snow
on my brow?' a letter says. 'Children, I so much miss you,

I kiss you all and your mother.' And me:
'How beautiful it would have been for you to have been here too!'

'Sell everything you can', he urged, 'send the children to school.'
'Do not despair, I might be coming home soon.'

*

We hung onto those few words that could cross
the clay-like murky territories between us.

These letters were like skin that covered
and protected our bodies from the cold outside,

each word a capillary that carried and supported
the life in each one of us. Each word was limitless,

clothed our souls and warmed against despair,
shielded us from *their* world of terror,

transported chills, shivers, anger, warmth
from us to Father, and back from him to us:

they took us to each other as we were.
When the censor took our words and talked *about* them,

discarded our handwriting and wrote *his*,
he became a flaying instrument.

Letters we sent were not received
(until now, thirty years on).

We, Marsyas the Satyr tied to our tree.
The Censor scraped at capillaries of our words,

what survives is howling: 'A year has passed with no news
from you'; 'Something awful is happening to you';

'No one looks after us anymore, they're all busy';
'Mother is ill and short tempered, even Grandmother has left';

'It's disgraceful that you have nothing to eat.'
Thirty years have gone and we have lived

with exposed wounds, doubts, fears, uncertainties.
Now I find the family letters from back then

in the midst of thousands of records.
I reconstruct the way we used to speak,

the way skin used to feel when it was still alive.
Denatured letters in the handwriting of the censor.

*

I make out capillaries under the flaying instrument,
I reconstruct parts of the skin from the words

that were copied out. We now know
what has been taken from us and how

words alone saved us then
and bring joy now, the joy of finding them,

for in their frail syllables I recognize the old self.
Apollo has cleaned his instrument and left.[9]

When we arrived at the Aiud prison, which figures in the poem and the files above, we were a largely healed family wandering into their past, trespassing in a sense into the private emotional territories of each other: my father experienced going through the line of visitors at the entrance of the prison, and we went on the other side of the visiting room, where he had vanished after our brief conversations with him in the 1980s. I wanted to see where he had been stretched on the walls, beaten and starved, where he spent years and years waiting for letters and packages from us which had seldom arrived, causing him to fear that we had abandoned him—something that came up again and again in the files with a blame that had only served to make us feel helpless. I wanted my father to be there with me, alive and well, to explain to me

---

[9] Carmen Bugan, 'A birthday letter', in *Releasing the Porcelain Birds* (Swindon: Shearsman, 2016), pp. 19–21.

the country we all had to leave. But I also decided to bring poetry with me, our family poetry, as I have come to think of it over the years. In my early twenties, after I learned English, I wrote a poem about visiting my father in this prison, and I published it in my first collection, *Crossing the Carpathians*. The poem is called 'Aiud'. I needed to bring that poem close to its source, so, when we arrived inside the prison, I made an audio recording of it, folding the present over the past as one voice: it felt like a triumph!

The next moment from that return trip to Romania concerns retracing my father's failed escape from the country. In 1965, in his mid-twenties, my father and his best friend tried to cross the Iron Curtain, the fortified ideological line that divided one Europe from the other during the Cold War. In 2010, I found the border police hand-drawn map of the Lesovo area in Bulgaria, about 400 meters from Turkey, complete with the haystacks in which they hid from police. Attached to the report was a list of the contents of my father's backpack when he was caught in the dead of winter. I also had the secret police reports of the escape journey from Romania, and we followed it faithfully, stopping to see each border, where he could replay his memories of events that took place 48 years earlier. In 2013, my father was just short of turning 80. Again, this was an emotional, painful moment and I was there as a writer who would cross the threshold in language from a private to a public utterance. Part of me hoped to write the poem for all those who perished trying to cross into a better world.

There was also the thrill of having somehow come through to the other side of the struggle, when we could enjoy the articulation, the clarity of freedom. As I sat down to write the poem 'A Walk on the Iron Curtain with My Father', I enjoyed staying focused on the words, on the rhythms of the language, on the minute details of the trip that evoked our emotional relationship. I hoped to give a sense of what the Iron Curtain stood for. This to me represents the notion of 'artistic distance'—the emotional distance from the subject of revisiting a profound loss—necessary to create writing focused on the event that takes place in language, in the spontaneous clinking of words that can only be heard in a state of stillness and tranquillity.

But here the poem depended on the bureaucracy of the files: the occasion of the poem had arisen because of the list of objects the border guards found in my father's backpack. That list is essentially an X-ray of his younger fugitive self in search of freedom, desperate and refusing to give up, giving up country and language but not giving up life itself. The poem is a trilogy: my father's younger self, his old self, and his child. And, of course, there is the hand-drawn map, which became the foggy morning landscape over Lesovo, and which I also put in the book. In this context the files have come to represent a backdrop of experience against which the poem was born. The language of oppression from the files has entered the fabric of the lyric language as one accepts the scar of a wound.

A walk with my father on the Iron Curtain

Arm in arm, my father and I return
to the ground of his failed escape:
it is now forty-eight years on.

The border between Romania
and Bulgaria at 110-111 point
is bathed in gold October light.

The maize silos where he slept are still here:
an old border guard curious to see us
loitering on the train tracks confirms Dad's memory,

as if History itself sent him our way
with the flock of geese and the red tractor
raising all the clamour in the peaceful morning.

It's a holy day for me, at my father's side,
with the map of his life, listening, listening
to the tempest in that night, icy rain, snow,

him and his friend inside the maize shelter
melting snow for tea, the horrifying days
when they searched the way with binoculars.

He ran to the other side of the world
with seventeen half-slices of salami,
a flashlight, and a dictionary,

some coins, probably more for good luck
than for anything they could buy, the shaver
for good looks, and a heart full of hope

We carry on past Negru Vodă:
Tolbukhin railway station, golden afternoon
and a wind that buffets us,

then Elhovo that looks more like a painting
with a dream worked inside the peeling blue
walls of the train station, my father, a puzzle

in changing light, seen through broken windows,
the coffee and baklava on the main street.
Arm in arm in the old quarters searching for his hotel

where he hid from police, the trap door that is
no longer there. Memory leads us off the map.
Then Lesovo in fog, like an elusive fish, the map

with the haystack where he slept to hide
from border guards, his hike along the roads
through the circular swamp, 400 meters from Turkey!

Ground of being on his ground of escape.
You cannot take the dreams away from anyone who dreams.
'I never thought I'd be back here as a free man', he says.

Here he is, the white in his hair, snowbells at temples,
the grey-green eyes, now wet, now dry, twinkling.
Locals watch us step off ghost trains at the disused station.[10]

Soaring Above the Pain: Rebecca Loncraine's *Skybound*

Among the writers who have understood language as a healing
resource and have managed to write 'above' their condition is the
biographer and memoirist Rebecca Loncraine.[11] I want to turn my
attention to her work in the context of the discussion of artistic
distance because her story is extremely private and personal and
she has avoided the risks so common for people writing about
their own illnesses: self-pity and sermonizing about suffering.
Her prose writing, at once reticent and poignant, has mined
the lyrical resources of language, gaining a unique perspective
on suffering and mortality: the physical perspective of flight,
of soaring above. This perspective offers a direct answer to the
question 'so what next?' which surfaces in relation to how we
talk about suffering.

Loncraine's fascination with being swept up in the sky began
in her early childhood on the family farm in the Black Mountains
of Wales, when she read *The Wizard of Oz*. Soon after finishing her
doctorate in literature at the University of Oxford, she went to

---

[10] Carmen Bugan, 'A walk with my father on the Iron Curtain', in *Releasing the Porcelain Birds* (Swindon: Shearsman, 2016), p. 41.

[11] An earlier draft of this discussion of *Skybound* has appeared as a review in *Harvard Review* Online on 8 May 2018, https://www.harvardreview.org/book-review/skybound/.

America to chase tornadoes and wrote a highly praised biography of L. Frank Baum. I met her when we were both at Oxford and enjoyed how naturally she brought scholarly research into her creative work, making her writing so focused and yet deeply felt. *Skybound,* her second book, moves through a history of engineless flight going all the way back to Leonardo da Vinci's notes in the *Codex on the Flight of Birds,* noting his drawing of an 'ornithopter', a 'machine with flapping wings'.[12] Loncraine also takes the reader on a tour of the skies that begins a few thousand feet above her childhood home and continues above New Zealand and Nepal before returning to one particular burnt side of a hill near her parents' farm.

From various heights, edging under the wings of magnificent birds and soaring far above mountain peaks that have remained inaccessible to most, Loncraine has crafted a language that helps her construct a map of her suffering: the view of the Alps on a flight map might look like an MRI scan of the landscape, while close to her childhood home, the hill with the burnt patch reminds her of her breast after radiation therapy. She returns to the landscape of her early life from above and understands it through new emotional and visual perspectives. Memories of her younger self growing up around the garden and the hills, surrounded by the rich song of birds, rise into consciousness as she soars above sheep and horses. She discovers the place of her family home in the larger logic of settlements within the landscape and from heights where the mountains and the glaciers begin to look like the backs

---

[12] Rebecca Loncraine, *Skybound* (London: Picador, 2018), p. 103.

of seals. As she travels up into the sky, she works to locate her own place in a world transformed by her illness.

Loncraine researched the geography of the places above which she flies and learned how people live there, and of their relationship to the environment. She studied the flora, the fauna, the shapes of rivers and lakes, and the structure of the winds and clouds above. When she walks on the ground, she is a botanist and the land-scape shimmers with the names and colours of flowers, herbs, and grasses. From inside her glider we see and feel a rich and variegated world, winds howling outside, while she and her flight instructor, Bo, find holes in the clouds to go up and down and around the sky. In the Black Mountains, she leaps above perfect rainbows, feeling like a child inside a drawing. In the Southern Alps of New Zealand, she is thrown about in turbulence that tests the strength of the glider and awakens within her that essential fear that makes her understand that she is fully alive: the illness hasn't dulled the thrill of being. Several months later, she feeds a rescue vulture with her hand from a paraglider near Pokhara in Nepal:

> He lands perfectly on my hand, decelerating from seventy kilo-meters an hour in a matter of seconds. He snatches the meat and then swoops off the gloved hand to the left and is swallowed again in the sky's currents, which have become as thick as water at this speed.[13]

The language of flight gives Loncraine a way to talk about the dev-astating effects of cancer and the gruelling treatment that pushed her to the edge. 'Trying to get some hold on fear', she says, 'is like circling over a mountain; it shape-shifts as you move, showing dramatically different sides from different points of view.'[14] At one

---

[13] Ibid., p. 284.   [14] Ibid., pp. 248–9.

point, she flies with the glider's guiding instruments covered up, so she can rely on her body to lead her through the mysterious and often dangerous skies. Her descriptions of lessons and flights are at once practical and utterly poetic: 'Like mastering an instrument, soaring requires a scientific understanding of the discipline, precision, hours and hours of practice, and total, passionate commitment...how to turn in the core of a thermal, how to recognize a convergence, katabatic winds, orographic clouds.'[15] Eventually flying is fluid, almost seamless: 'I have the sense now that the sky has crept up into my spine, worked its blue way into my bones.'[16]

Skybound is not a book only for cancer patients, though it certainly contains comfort and inspiration to keep going through awful treatments. In the deepest sense, the book is about the sheer thrill of being part of the astonishing Earth we have in common. The freshness of the imagery and the childlike joy of being in the sky recall another book, Selma Lagerlöf's *The Wonderful Adventures of Nils*, the story of an imaginary little boy who flies all over Sweden with the wild geese, and who has this conversation with a bird he meets during his journey:

> "If I weren't a raven, but just human like you, then I'd settle here and learn everything that is in books," said the raven. "Wouldn't you like to do that, too?"
>
> "Oh, no," said Nils. "I'd rather go around with the wild geese."[17]

Nils says this because, as we learn during our journey with him on the back of the snow goose, he learns wonderful things about his own condition and about the world at large: both in a physical

---

[15] Ibid., pp. 202–4.   [16] Ibid., p. 210.
[17] Selma Lagerlöf, *The Wonderful Adventures of Nils*, trans. Joan Tate (Edinburgh: Floris Books, 1992), p. 52.

and in a metaphorical sense. Only by flying above the landscape of his country (and metaphorically, above his own preoccupations) does he learn about the ways, hardships, and the joys of others. Most importantly, he learns the rewards of being helpful, needed, and recognized by others as a worthwhile being. Aside from performing the function of a geography school primer, the story of Nils offers the view that one becomes richer and can experience personal healing by seeing oneself in the world, rather than in complete isolation. One learns how to be oneself by being with others: this is a great insight especially for the contemporary writer in a conflict-riven world.

Rebecca Loncraine died in 2016, shortly after finishing *Skybound*. In the final images of her story, we find her sleeping at home under the stars by which she can tell seasons and the time of the night as they move above the trees and behind the barn. We see her in the dawn chorus, which is perceived as 'a river of birdsong; I see it flowing past in my mind's eye as I fall back into a doze with the delicious sensation of floating on a stream of song'.[18] There is depth and clarity in this acknowledgement that life is coming to an end; it is a book written against delusion, against despair, and also against rigid silence. Like Dante's vision that becomes sharper with looking, so her vision is becoming clearer—about her own journey in life, about her mortality, about the way language has imparted its light to her as she changed while flying and writing about it. What could have been an expression of self-indulgent fear of dying has become an expression of strength, what could have been a denial has become a face-to-face confrontation.

[18] Loncraine, *Skybound*, p. 260.

Loncraine's work evidences principles of engaging terror that I believe can be used also by the poet who writes about social and political oppression. The effects of public oppression are similar to those of physical and mental illness, analogous to those of abuse at the hands of family and friends: we fall silent, we feel powerless, we think that there is no way to overcome the burdens placed on us, we fear, and more importantly, we find the language to maintain those narratives. Loncraine draws on clarity of expression and on our ability to view suffering from several perspectives, in order to understand its inevitability together with the need to resist it. Reading her book, several years after I returned from my own journey through the Romanian prisons and the Iron Curtain with my family, I reflected on the ways in which that journey opened to me, and opened me to the larger context of human suffering in tyrannical regimes, and on how much we are willing to sacrifice in order to be understood as human beings with the need to breathe freely on this Earth.

'Grief' as 'Honest and Vibrant Enterprise': Hisham Matar's *The Return*

I'd like to discuss the use of poetic language in memoir a little further, this time in the context of political oppression, as it affects familial bonds. The writer Hisham Matar has spent most of his adult life not knowing whether his dissident father is dead or alive.[19] At one anniversary marking his disappearance, the family gathered

---

[19] This discussion of Hisham Matar's memoir, in an earlier version, was published in *Harvard Review* Online on 15 June 2017, https://www.harvardreview.org/book-review/the-return-fathers-sons-and-the-land-in-between/.

in the 'surrogate' city of Nairobi, whose earth he describes as 'an inkwell' and 'told and retold the story of how it had happened'.[20] Just days later, everyone flew home to a different country.

Matar has won the Pulitzer Prize in autobiography/biography for his memoir *The Return*, described by the committee as 'a first-person elegy for home and father that examines with controlled emotion the past and present of an embattled region'. Born in New York City to Libyan parents, Matar divided his childhood between Tripoli and Cairo, was educated in England, and has enjoyed success from the outset of his literary career with two novels. His memoir, both a chronicle of private family pain and a historical account of life under Gaddafi, creates a space for reflection on freedom and humanity. As a piece of literature, it reminds one of Milosz's conviction about poetry: it is 'on the side of being and against nothingness'. The prose often reads like a long poem and I think it is this evocative aspect of language that helps carry the experience to the heart of the reader.

Twenty-two years after Jaballa Matar, one of Gaddafi's most vocal opponents, vanished into the Abu Salim prison, his son Hisham Matar took his wife and mother to Libya to find him. His voice reverberates with pride for his father's courage, the years of fruitless search for information about his disappearance, and exile. We follow Matar to a changed and changing Benghazi and see him visiting a deeply wounded but resilient extended family who gather together over fragrant meals, memories, poetry, and innumerable cups of tea in houses, apartments, and in the other-worldly desert. We meet Matar's dissident grandfather, who opens

---

[20] Hisham Matar, *The Return: Fathers, Sons, and the Land in Between* (New York: Random House, 2016), p. 195.

his shirt to show the place where a bullet entered his body. His house reflects the architecture of his character, and his character is like his long poems: 'austere, unpredictable, plain, unfinished, yet inhabited'.[21] Matar's mother houses and feeds women whose sons and husbands had joined the resistance and were incarcerated in the same prison as Jaballa Matar. We learn the story of a woman who spent years delivering monthly packages of food and toiletries to her son, unaware that he had been murdered in the prison where she had been accepting the guards' varied excuses for not granting her a visit.

Libya is seen through the eyes of its estranged son who longs for the sea, who meditates on the architecture trampled by invaders, who has known other countries, who is buffeted by his native Arabic and the English language in which he now writes. Yet the quest of the book remains Jaballa Matar: the father, the inspirational leader, the writer, the poet, the prisoner, the disappeared. Jaballa becomes larger than life, the symbol of telling truth to power and at the same time the painfully absent father. It is through this dual image of father-hero that the story of political brutality is told. To Matar, the absence of his father 'has never seemed empty or passive but rather a busy place, vocal and insistent'.[22] He carves into language to shape this absence, to express the loss of his father, and in turn records a loss within himself, saying: 'I do not have a grammar for him.' 'Grief', he explains, is 'an active and vibrant enterprise. It is hard honest work. It can break your back.'[23] For him, this grief enters words themselves.

---

[21] Ibid., pp. 127–8.
[22] Ibid., p. 144.   [23] Ibid., p. 145.

What gives his book a special place in the literature of witness is the full employment of lyric language in order to intimate the ravages of history, the cruelty and indifference of the powerful, and to find solace in art, nature, and family. Gaddafi and his son are portrayed through the monstrosity of their actions. The language goes beyond Matar's personal story to that place of conscience where his torment becomes an occasion for self-examination. To those families who stood up for freedom and have paid for it with prison and exile, Matar's book is the place where they can recognize a similar loss. His words traverse territories of languages and cultures and bring into the consciousness of literature a Jaballa Matar who will not disappear. Of the Libyan political prisoners he encounters, Matar says something achingly familiar to those who fight oppression everywhere: 'They wanted to bring me into the darkness, to expose the suffering and, in doing so, discreetly and indirectly emphasize the momentous achievement of having survived it. Is there an achievement greater than surviving suffering? Of coming through mostly intact?'[24] Faced with impossible situations—cancer diagnosis, losing a parent, or constant hardship—most of us will search for ways to break through them, and lyric language can be an ally that can provide the inner strength with which we can proceed.

Conclusion: The Artistic Principle of Sanity

Language is thrilling, and dangerous. Political upheaval, the stories we tell ourselves as we obey authority, or as we accept destructive

---

[24] Ibid., p. 225.

situations in our private lives, the words we tell ourselves to justify participating in the pain of others, or ignoring it, can be as disorienting as madness. I have spent several years researching the ways in which other poets have dealt with their own histories, with the conflicting politics of their own countries, and have articulated the notion of a poetics of artistic distance in relation to them. In my book on *Seamus Heaney and East European Poetry in Translation: Poetics of Exile*, I have argued that Seamus Heaney, Osip Mandelstam, Czeslaw Milosz, Joseph Brodsky, and Zbigniew Herbert did not flinch in the face of historical turmoil, but that their fidelity to form has remained, because they believed that their contribution to their history needed to remain artistic, maintaining the vigour of language. Their work calls to mind the sacrifice the poets make as they defend poetry when society demands that they produce works that participate in political discourse. Yet for me it is not a question of needing to split myself between a responsibility to witness and a responsibility to obey the artistic imperative. For me, writing has involved taking denatured language and turning it into a language that cleans the wounds. The poetics I have adopted in *Releasing the Porcelain Birds: Poems After Surveillance* is a poetics of quotation marks, where the language of oppression enters into the language of poetry, as I use one in order to stare down the other.

I return to my initial questions: How to talk about suffering? How to give an intimation of it without cheapening the language into self-pity, or begging for the pity of the reader, or inflicting agony on the reader, or turning it into propaganda? Self-absorbed poetry, as honest and as eloquent as it may be in saying 'I suffer', doesn't rise beyond itself, it only mirrors itself. As writers, we can afford to step aside from our own pain—and passions—just enough so that at the end of the poem the reader feels what Wilfred Owen called 'the pity of War', knowing that 'the poetry is in the pity',[25] and hopefully beyond it, to the realization that the cruelty people inflict on one another is actually something which *can* be controlled, because it is possible to avoid becoming slaves of our own anger and fear. We do not have agency over mortality, terminal illness, and political upheaval, but we have *some* agency over how we engage with our social and political problems in the language of poetry. We can write ourselves free, the pen is in our hand.

How, as writers, we place ourselves in relation to those problems, rather than inside them, is the difficult task ahead. Those of us who write, exercise control over language, and should know the difference between freedom and licence, between self-control and servitude, between language that soothes and language that causes more pain. This requires as much thinking as feeling. Writers work with feelings but they also work with ideas, and I would like to call attention here to a lecture on two kinds of liberty by Sir Isaiah Berlin, where he explains the role of ideas and the power of personal agency in achieving freedom. 'Ideas', says Berlin, 'are of interest solely so far as they constitute problems or answers to problems which arise in the course of men's reflection about their place and their purpose in the world, and the nature of that world, and their own relationship with it.'[26] Writers, who are uniquely placed to engage with people's 'reflection' about

---

[25] Wilfred Owen, 'Preface', in *The Collected Poems of Wilfred Owen*, ed., Edmund Blunden (New York: New Directions, 1965).

[26] Isaiah Berlin, 'Two Concepts of Liberty' (Original dictation A), in The Isaiah Berlin Virtual Library, Wolfson College, Oxford University, Oxford, UK, http://berlin.wolf.ox.ac.uk/published_works/tcl/tcl-a.pdf [167, 168].

themselves in the world, often offer ideas that position and reposition the individual in relation to the world. Here I would like to discuss how inner freedom and political freedom illuminate and strengthen each other in a way analogous to Dante's perception of the light as clearer the more he looked upon it, as it shone on him.

The central issue concerning political theory, according to Berlin, is obedience: why should anyone obey authority instead of doing what one wants? The central problem, according to him is coercion, which he defines as 'the deprivation of freedom'.[27] Freedom 'in a political sense' is defined by him in two ways, which I find relevant to my discussion about the role of the writer in relation to suffering. The first sense of freedom has to do with an absence of resistance from the society, so that one feels unconstrained from doing as one pleases. This, Berlin calls 'negative liberty' because the individual is not required to make a choice, since no one is interfering in his or her actions—one lives without being coerced, or prevented by another person, or by a government, from attaining his or her goal. This, of course, must be considered in terms of the social contract which requires trading certain forms of freedom for others, as I discussed in Chapter 2 of this book. The second sense of liberty is 'positive' because it involves a choice on the part of the individual in society, a choice which requires self-mastery. The positive sense of liberty answers the question of who is in charge when constraints are imposed— in Berlin's words, 'What is the source of control, when it exists, which can prevent someone from doing what he wishes?'[28] The answer to this question is 'oneself': Berlin places high importance on self-governance so that 'This desire to be self-directed has,

[27] Ibid, p. 3.   [28] Ibid., p. 4.

historically, taken two major forms: the first, that of self-denial to attain independence; the second, that of conquest of obstacles in my path to attain the same end.'[29] Self-denial, as explained by Berlin, requires one to relinquish the desires for that which one cannot have and to retreat into the inner self. It is an extreme form of self-abnegation, which Berlin calls 'the doctrine of sour grapes'.[30] As human beings, we desire to be 'recognized' by others so that we may feel understood: 'this understanding creates' in the individual, argues Berlin, 'the sense of being somebody, and not nobody...in the world'.[31] Freedom is then understood through the willingness to be governed by someone or something of one's choice, on the mutual recognition of individual humanity. This recognition of individual humanity cannot be relinquished if one is to feel free.

And it is here that the work of the writer flourishes: in the continual questioning, illumination, presentation, imagination of what it is to be recognized by others as a human being who will be treated with dignity. To cite Berlin again: 'The power of choosing between incompatible, equally absolute alternatives is one of the characteristics that make human beings human. The value of the act of choosing lies in itself, not as a means to something else.'[32] Berlin's view on liberty is thus as follows:

> The extent of my liberty to choose as I desire must be weighed against the claims of other values – equality or justice, or happiness, or whatever other ends men or societies may have set their hearts upon. Moreover it will be curtailed by the claims of other persons to an equal measure of liberty, which must be respected not because of some logical principle whereby liberty for one man

---

[29] Ibid., p. 15. [30] Ibid., p. 22.
[31] Ibid., p. 28. [32] Ibid., p. 36.

necessarily entails belief in the liberty of others, but as a claim for justice or equality of similar claims, a moral end in itself.[33]

This brings us to the concept of emotional and intellectual self-mastery required to attain artistic distance. Charles Lamb best expressed the concept of artistic distance, and one phrase of his rings true for me every time I return to the language of oppression as the material of my poetry. Lamb explains that when the wits of the writers 'wander' even a little

> from nature or actual existence, they lose themselves, and their readers…They do not create, which implies shaping and consistency. Their imaginations are not active—for to be active is to call something into shape and form—but passive, as men in sick dreams.

This passage occurs in his short piece called 'Sanity of True Genius' in *The Essays of Elia*. I find his definition of imagination as calling something into shape and form beneficial: this is useful, and simple, and clear-headed. I will quote here another part of his essay:

> The greatness of wit, by which the poetic talent is here chiefly to be understood, manifests itself in the admirable balance of all the faculties. Madness is the disproportionate straining or excess of any one of them…men, finding in the raptures of higher poetry a condition of exaltation, to which they have no parallel in their own experience, besides the spurious resemblance of it in dreams and fevers, impute a state of dreaminess and fever to the poet. But the true poet dreams being awake. He is not possessed by his subject, but has dominion over it.[34]

---

[33] Ibid., p. 36.

[34] Charles Lamb, 'Sanity of true genius', in *The Essays of Elia* (London: Thomas Nelson & Sons, [1823–33] 2013), pp. 255–7.

I believe that only when the 'poet dreams being awake' and thus acquires 'dominion' over the 'subject', is it possible to invest the work with the moral worth Berlin talks about, where values are not dictated by immediate and topical interests but by their immutability and permanence which guide our actions. Writing about true events that have affected, and continue to affect, the lives of people requires a very clear sense of responsibility to the factual, as such writing essentially portrays one life in a historical moment. And because the story has been lived already and the facts have been recorded, there is no room for any artistic licence, no room for plot twists and climax, no room for characterization, or the surprise of hyperbole. But we experience each historical event, each historical trauma, in our own individual and private way, we see the larger events by how they affect us, personally. Indeed, very few—if any—have the eagle-eye's view on the spider web of the world's problems. The opportunity for literature is to make space for the individual, the unacknowledged, the marginalized, and the ordinary, to enrich that account of history: one family at the time, one censored letter at the time, one cancer diagnosis at the time.

There is great potential in writing a poem about the letters that were in fact written and sent, and that the person on the other side of the prison walls cared, even if that discovery comes thirty years on. A poem can find a way of expressing that surprise and joy, and so it would be a poem of love, and the story would be a story of faithful love which had survived the waves of history. At the end of the *Divine Comedy*, we find the poet changed from a figure who started out lost in the woods, to someone who has reached joy. Dante finds in the light 'l'amor che move il sole e l'altre stelle':

'The Love, which moves the sun and the other stars.'[35] This, to me, is a sensible way to look at the relationship between writer and language, as it incorporates the experience and the language of oppression. Healing can be generated in the rhythms and incantations of words, both for the one who writes, and for the reader, who will recognize a sense of form, harmony, and respect for human life. I will end with four lines from the sonnet 'The Instant' by Jorge Luis Borges (translated by Alastair Reid) which sums up what I have tried to argue in this chapter:

> Between dawn and nightfall is an abyss
> of agonies, felicities, and cares.
> The face that looks back from the wasted mirrors,
> the mirrors of night, is not the same face.[36]

[35] Dante Alighieri, *The Divine Comedy: Paradiso*, vol. 1, Text, trans. Charles S. Singleton (Princeton, NJ: Princeton University Press, 1975), p. 380.
[36] Jorge Luis Borges, 'The Instant', in *The Sonnets (English and Spanish)*, ed., Stephen Kessler (New York: Penguin Books, 2010), p. 81.

5

WRITING IN TURBULENT TIMES

Every generation has its soul-searching moments, when redis-covering difficult aspects of the past is key to the process of self-examination and ascertaining the legacy of historical trauma. Between the Covid-19 pandemic, the renewed concerns over racism and inequality, and the deepening climate crisis, we are experiencing a significant period in our history as a global community, when we are compelled to meditate on the human cost of our choices. This brings upon a deeper reflection on the relationship between civilization and oppression, and perhaps it is useful to remind ourselves of the remarks made by Miguel de Unamuno in his book, *The Tragic Sense of Life*:

> Civilization began on the day on which one man, by subjecting another to his will and compelling him to do the work for two, was enabled to devote himself to the contemplation of the world and to set his captive upon works of luxury. It was slavery than enabled Plato to speculate upon the ideal republic, and it was war that brought slavery about. Not without reason was Athena the goddess of war and of wisdom. But is there any need to repeat once again these obvious truths, which, though they have continually been forgotten, are continually rediscovered?[1]

[1] Miguel de Unamuno, *The Tragic Sense of Life*, trans. J.E. Crawford Flitch (New York: Dover Publications, 1954), p. 280.

Poetry and the Language of Oppression: Essays on Politics and Poetics. Carmen Bugan, Oxford University Press (2021). © Carmen Bugan. DOI: 10.1093/oso/9780198868323.003.0006

The importance of reminding ourselves of 'obvious truths', especially those that reveal the foundations of civilization, cannot be overstated. Many are beginning to reread literature for its own tales of salvation and downfalls, and, even more importantly, for its portrayal of civilization. The writer who engages with oppression must use language as precisely and as skilfully as a surgeon uses the knife: whatever cut must be made, it must be a part of the curative process.

Nowadays there is both a political and politicized outlook of literature, as entirely distinct from its significance 'as a form of resistance', or as Heaney has put it, as an expression of 'solidarity with the doomed'.[2] Contemporary injustice and oppression, as well as the abhorrence of such things not only find their expressions in language but are perpetuated by language. The creative writer is in a unique position to question, reimagine, discover and rediscover how language works, in an attempt to sustain the values that hold humankind together.

Writing about public duress entails certain risks, the most dangerous being the presumption that one person is capable of understanding the energies of the culture and society, and somehow can function as the speaker of collective consciousness, especially at times when so many communities in particular societies are in conflict and competing for power. For this reason, writing

---

[2] Seamus Heaney, 'The Interesting Case of Nero, Chekhov's Cognac and a Knocker', in *Government of the Tongue: Selected Prose 1978–1987* (New York: Farrar, Straus and Giroux, 1988). He writes: 'The shorthand name we have evolved for this figure is the "poet as witness", and he represents poetry's solidarity with the doomed, the deprived, the victimized, the under-privileged. The witness is any figure in whom the truth-telling urge and the compulsion to identify with the oppressed become necessarily integral with the act of writing itself.' (p. XVI).

necessitates deep reflection on the place the individual occupies in society, the nature of freedom, the sense of civic responsibility, and the uses and abuses of ordinary and literary language. Poetry is to be valued precisely because its readers can recognize themselves and their human condition in the emotional, spiritual, and intellectual fabric of the poem. Poetry succeeds in speaking 'heart to heart' through images, music, and figurative language which render the harsh reality with precision, while creating a protected, reflective space for the mind. So, how does the poet become attuned to the language of the world's upheaval? What is the appropriate expressive language that is at once *dulce et utile*, as Horace would have it? Furthermore, to what extent should the contemporary poet consider the demographics of literary readership in order to achieve that 'solidarity with the doomed'?

The Princeton Encyclopedia of Poetry and Poetics defines political poetry thus: 'Political poems concern situations that might be otherwise. Causes and consequences, choices—these are the special concerns of political poets.' It defines political verse as:

> Gr. *Politikos stichos*, the verse of the polis and its citizens. A Byzantine meter of 15 syllables, accentually based on iambic. First appears in 10th century A.D. and is the standard meter for Mod. Greek Poetry from at least the 12th c. to the present day.[3]

This chapter investigates whether literature that engages with politics is, or indeed should be, 'political', and in what sense. It also asks whether the poet, in dealing with the world of inner feelings in the context of public emotion has an opportunity to question

---

[3] Robert von Hallberg, 'Politics and Poetry', in *The New Princeton Encyclopedia of Poetry and Poetics*, ed. Alex Preminger and T.V.F. Brogan (Princeton, NJ: Princeton University Press, 1993), pp. 960–4 (961); see also 'Political Verse', p. 960.

our foundational understanding of what makes us civilized, or uncivilized, and what we mean by an 'examination of language'. Furthermore, it turns attention to the defining characteristics of power narratives in the literature about oppression, focusing on how they expose the oppressor, enabling the oppressed to resist.

During the course of the present book I have considered the language of oppression, located the interface between poetry and politics, and discussed writing in a non-native language from the point of view of a poet who makes a personal testimony, while writing herself free. The personal aspect of experience has been emphasized so that the contact with political language is understood as part of the normal course of life, rather than a poetic incursion into political realities for the purpose of championing particular political ideas. Making a personal testimony in poetry requires awareness of the dangers of the suggestive. There needs to be a very precise balance in the poem that is a personal utterance about a shared public trauma: the voice must remain entirely one's own as it joins the public grief, so that it presents the individual while it paints the larger situation truthfully. But should poetry born in a turbulent time participate in partisan politics? What is the difference between poetry that is *profoundly* political and simple verse propaganda? What is the role of imagination in literature that deals with a troubling historical reality? How does figurative language affect the way we experience public conflict? To put it another way, what claims can we make for poetry in troubled times? And at what point does lyric language break under sustained pressure?

In his book, *Language and Silence*, George Steiner devotes a section to Marxism and literature, acknowledging the profound influence communism had on many of the major writers, critics, and philosophers of the last century and beyond. His essay, 'The Writer and Communism' ends with a question which is at the heart of my work: 'Where do we cross the line between the artist as conveyor of the ideals of his society and the artist as the maker of mere propaganda?'[4] Though the question is left open, it seems to me that he hinted at the complicated political relationship between a writer and his time, when he expressed irritation with the standard reading of George Orwell's 1984 as an allegory of Cold War totalitarianism:

> 1984 is not…a parable of the totalitarian rule of Stalin, Hitler, and Mao Tse-tung. The polemic of the fable is not unilinear. Orwell's critique bears simultaneously on the police state and on capitalist consumer society, with its illiteracy of values and its conformities. "Newspeak," the language of Orwell's nightmare, is both the jargon of dialectical materialism and the verbiage of commercial advertisement and mass-media…Our own acquisitive society appalled him. He noted in it germs of inhumanity comparable to those endemic in Stalinism…To make 1984 a pamphlet in the intellectual cold war is to misread and diminish the book.[5]

This defence of 1984 could not be more prescient: Steiner died in 2020 and he must have shuddered at the culture that produced Donald Trump, and at Kellyanne Conway's use of the term 'alternative reality' at her presidential press briefings. George Orwell's novel went to the top of the bestseller charts in the United States following the election of Trump in 2016. 1984 is certainly a political book if we view politics in literature beyond their use as mere

---

[4] George Steiner, Language and Silence: Essays on Language, Literature and the Inhuman (New York: Atheneum, 1972), p. 364.

[5] Ibid., p. 361.

partisanship: the book creates an imaginary world that indicts any abusive political system. What Steiner says about the book is fundamental to the understanding of the term 'political' I raise here in relation to literature, and especially poetry: it's not political one-sidedness (of which every writer is at risk) but politics in the sense of reassessing how we govern ourselves with language. A writer is profoundly political when his or her work exposes manipulation and coercion through language. George Orwell's novel is not a weapon to fight communism, but a warning about the various, and often creative, pernicious forms of oppression. Crimes against humanity are just as foul, whether they are committed by Hitler, Stalin, or multinational corporations. Though the line between the artist as 'conveyor of ideals' and the artist 'as maker of mere propaganda' is extremely thin, it's still quite visible. I would like to stand on this line for the duration of this chapter, to acknowledge the difficulties of writing about one's ethical stance when writing is provoked by major political currents.

Like other members of society, poets and writers are shaped by their times. Their language takes on not only the colouring but also the character of the experience, and is thus identified with a particular historical moment. For example, speaking about the circumstances at the end of the Second World War, the poet Salvatore Quasimodo acknowledged:

> War, I have always said, forces men to change their standards, regardless of whether their country has won or lost. Poetics and philosophies disintegrate "when the trees fall and the walls collapse". At the point when continuity was interrupted by the first nuclear explosion, it would have been too easy to recover the formal sediment which linked us with an age of poetic decorum, of a preoccupation with poetic sounds. After the turbulence of death,

moral principles and even religious proofs are called into question. Men of letters who cling to the private successes of their petty aesthetics shut themselves off from poetry's restless presence.[6]

They key point Quasimodo makes in his Nobel Prize lecture is about 'poetry's restless presence': its ability to generate a language that is fully present to the moment of transformation, when we rethink how we live our lives. Necessary changes take place in poetic form, tone, and he argues that these changes provide a continuity of poetic tradition rather than a break from it. 'Expressive' and 'pragmatic' poetics ('the poetics of feelings and the poetics of action') are brought together to yield a language that reflects our personal and collective encounter with history.

But 'poetry of the time' (as we might call it) does not have to remain pinned to the political currents in circulation when it was written—like a dead butterfly in a glass case. One does not read Pablo Neruda simply as a communist poet and Osip Mandelstam as an anti-Stalinist, even though what animates much of their poetry was born in these political situations and both poets were willing to suffer for their convictions. They wrote to repel injustice, and I am convinced that they would have stood against many terrible political situations unfolding in our own time, because of their principles. One reads Neruda for his exuberant language and Mandelstam for his lament of solitude: in other words, for the consequences that political turbulence brings to what I call 'the language within language' that constitutes poetry. Even deeper than this 'reading for contributions to language', their poetry

---

[6] Salvatore Quasimodo, 'The Poet and the Politician', Nobel Lecture, NobelPrize.org. Nobel Media AB 2020, 4 May 2020, https://www.nobelprize.org/prizes/literature/1959/quasimodo/lecture/.

gained appreciation for its illuminating expressions of feelings. It's unlikely that these poets' work will turn their readers into members of any political party: it neither is nor is meant to function as propaganda. The triumph of poetry written under pressure is that it indicates the health of our species, that is, its potential to recognize and survive its mistakes, its potential to look forward. This is why it is not sufficient to think of poetry only in terms of its artistic qualities, or only of its use to society. We must also think of poetry in terms of its spiritual potential, its access to our deeper self through its fundamental moral articulations.[7]

The protest tradition remains grounded in one view of politics or another and the political idiom lends coarseness to the language of poetry. Political poems are at risk of being read as banners and posters. True success depends on the use of figurative language in order to confront reality (to place it in the larger perspective of human experience) as much as on the accurate depiction of reality as a means to challenge figurative language (so that imagination does not become an escape from experience). One of the difficulties I have encountered when writing about extreme poverty on the streets of wealthy cities, and most recently about the Covid-19 pandemic and the Black Lives Matter protests has been a proneness to rely too much on the particular images that best identified the specific impact these events had on me: the homeless living on the streets, refrigerated trucks, people waiting at food distribution centres, mass graves, police aiming their guns at protesters, and

---

[7] William Wordsworth had anticipated this assertion, writing that the poets' thoughts, feelings, and passions are 'connected...with our moral sentiments and animal sensations, and with the causes which excite these...with...gratitude and hope'. See William Wordsworth, 'Preface to *Lyrical Ballads*', in *The Norton Anthology of English Literature*, Sixth Edition, ed., M.H. Abrams (New York: W.W.W. Norton, 1993), p. 151.

the images of cities in flames. Here is a poem about Penn Station, New York, where I was concerned with the loss of dignity in old age because of poverty:

Penn Station, NY, January 23

He must be about eighty years old
And looks glad for the warmth
Of the crowded corridors filled with smells
Of food, luggage, and strong perfume.

He sits at the next table holding a garbage bag,
Takes out a box at a time, a wrap at a time,
Licks the crumbs and makes a pile of paper
Next to his right hand. Some seaweed, a bite

Of rice fallen from a sushi, a piece of noodle.
No one minds him, they look at their boxes
Filled with raw fish and ginger, check their phones,
The music from the restaurant plays on.

He smells like garbage. His eyes are warm
But resigned. The crumbs make a meagre meal,
So when he finishes going through the wraps,
He starts all over from the stack of empty boxes,

As if opening them again and again
Will make the food appear, the way we replay
A memory hoping the rehearsal will
Divine a treasured moment, and bring it back.

When he is convinced nothing is left, he carries the stack
To the large bin that had been just emptied.
He takes a napkin from the supply station, returns
To his place at the table, and wipes it clean.[8]

---

[8] Carmen Bugan, 'Penn Station, NY, January 23', in *Lilies from America: New and Selected Poems* (Swindon: Shearsman Books, 2019), p. 111.

WRITING IN TURBULENT TIMES

With the most recent poems about the pandemic and the protests about racial injustice, while I was able to put the worries about political commitment to one side, I could not ignore the worry that the poems might not be understood outside the specific references to their context. The linguistic decisions I made had to balance the specificity of images before my eyes with the imagery that transcends the particulars: the frailty of the human body, the fear of death, the dread of authority even in a democracy, the lack of trust in people and institutions. I felt a deep need to return to the limpid, clear-headed resources of language, so these poems are written in very plain speech indeed; they are still 'unfinished' to warrant inclusion in a book at the present time. Milosz's lines from 'Calling to order', 'You could scream/ Because mankind is mad',[9] his poetics in 'In a buggy at dusk' where 'the goal of an artist' is 'to be free from violent joys and sorrows',[10] and his exhortation to the oppressed in 'Dedication', 'You whom I could not save/ Listen to me', while admitting that he could offer only 'this simple speech as I would be ashamed of another', because 'there is in me no wizardry of words'[11] appealed to me profoundly as I considered what my voice could sound out in the unfolding public grief.

Meena Alexander's 'Invisible Grammar'

The successful poem, alive with the 'restless presence' Quasimodo talks about has the same effect on the reader as feeling the pulse of

---

[9] Czeslaw Milosz, 'Calling to order', in *New and Collected Poems 1931–2001*, trans. Czeslaw Milosz and Lilian Vallee (New York: Allen Lane, 2001), p. 271.

[10] Czeslaw Milosz, 'In a buggy at dusk', in *New and Collected Poems 1931–2001*, trans. Czeslaw Milosz and Robert Hass, p. 488.

[11] Czeslaw Milosz, 'Dedication', in *New and Collected Poems 1931–2001*, trans. Czeslaw Milosz , p. 77.

blood through the veins—it's warm, impossible to miss. Certain poets are able to register the living humanity in all its insecurity, self-doubt, but also respect and joy for life. Here I shall turn for an example to the poetry of Meena Alexander, who has questioned honestly the sufficiency of poetic language to meet the suffering of others, and writes convincingly about the poet's need to reconcile with the truth. Meena Alexander's wide-ranging collection *Atmospheric Embroidery* raises important questions about how much poetry can help us to understand the suffering of others.[12]

Alexander was born in India and lived in the U.S. for the last quarter-century of her life, but she also spent time in several other countries, including Sudan and England. One of the best-known Indian poets in America, the poet made her mark by writing about dislocation and transformation of body, history, and experience; she also published novels, criticism and a memoir, *Fault Lines*. In a 2005 interview in *The Kenyon Review*, Alexander spoke of her belief that 'In a time of violence, the task of poetry is in some way to reconcile us to our world and to allow us a measure of tenderness and grace with which to exist.'[13] *Atmospheric Embroidery* answers this call, but not without showing the limitations of the lyric and of language as it engages with the world's horrors. In 'Night Theater', she laments, 'We have no words / for what is happening.'[14] The

---

[12] A slightly different version of this discussion of Meena Alexander's work has appeared as a review of her poetry collection, *Atmospheric Embroidery* in *Harvard Review* Online on 11 April 2019, https://www.harvardreview.org/book-review/atmospheric-embroidery/.

[13] Ruth Maxey, 'An interview with Meena Alexander', *The Kenyon Review*, Winter 2006. Accessed 7 July 2020, https://kenyonreview.org/journal/winter-2006/selections/an-interview-with-meena-alexander/.

[14] Meena Alexander, 'Night theater', in *Atmospheric Embroidery* (Evanston, IL: TriQuarterly Books, 2018), p. 43.

speaker in the poem 'Fragment in Praise of the Book' suggests that the 'Book with the word for love / In all the languages that flow through me' is also the 'Book of alphabets burnt so the truth can be told.'[15]

In particular, Alexander expresses doubts that language can represent incoherence and brutality. In 'Chilika Lake', where girls 'will float in the warmth of lake water / Gone to hell for love, nothing but' and where a village is a scene of 'carnage of crows / Hurried betrothals behind cheap mauve curtains', the past is seen as 'Festoons of words no one believes.'[16] In 'Last Colors' a nameless, genderless child draws pictures of a father who lies in Khartoun with his hands and ears torn, and of a 'woman with a scarlet face, / Arms outstretched, body flung into blue.'[17] Alexander creates a nightmarish world where the violence that the child draws has clear and abundant representation in the poem, but where there is no representation of the child who has witnessed it all. 'Last Colors' is part of a cycle written in response to drawings made by children from Darfur living in relief camps on the Chad border. The cycle's opening poem, 'Sand Music', speaks in the voices of the camp children, who in turn speak for all people dislocated by unimaginable violence: 'We do not know who we are or what songs we might sing.'[18] In this line, Alexander points again to what is left unvoiced and unpainted, and calls into question the power of art to witness. Many of the poems do not imagine the faces, the

---

[15] Meena Alexander, 'Fragment in praise of the book', in *Atmospheric Embroidery*, p. 42.

[16] Meena Alexander, 'Chilika Lake', in *Atmospheric Embroidery*, p. 44.

[17] Meena Alexander, 'Last colors', in *Atmospheric Embroidery*, p. 39.

[18] Meena Alexander, 'Sand music', in *Atmospheric Embroidery*, p. 35.

features, the names of the children whose drawings have inspired their existence. The reader sees the horrors, but not the individuals experiencing them. I see this as an acknowledgement that we cannot ever imagine the lives of those oppressed, an act of humility in the face of suffering many of us will not know.

However, in the poem 'Nurredin' we have a child speaking in the first person, naming himself, urging the reader to 'Remember me, Nurredin / My name means light of day.'[19] Alexander also links the materiality of language and the body of the woman who suffers abuse, both merging in one voice which says, 'I am your language, do not cover me',[20] expressing thus the idea that with violence and violation of the people, language is mutilated as well. She calls us to witness the downfall of civilization. And yet, even as language falters, the speaker of the opening poem 'Aesthetic Knowledge' reassures us that 'An invisible grammar holds us in place.'[21] Alexander creates her own grammar, which holds past and present in three continents, and places personal stories of love and loss in a conflict-riven world. 'The Journey' is a beautiful indication of how language and experience come together to show the complexity of the poet's work:

> There were many languages flowing in the fountain
> In spite of certain confusion I decided not to stay thirsty.[22]

[19] Meena Alexander, 'Nurredin', in *Atmospheric Embroidery*, p. 38.
[20] Meena Alexander, 'Green Leaves of El Fasher', in *Atmospheric Embroidery*, p. 37.
[21] Meena Alexander, 'Aesthetic knowledge', in *Atmospheric Embroidery*, p. 3.
[22] Meena Alexander, 'The journey', in *Atmospheric Embroidery*, p. 32.

Atmospheric Embroidery also contains poems about the 'periodic pleasure / Of small happenings' as in 'Darling Coffee' in which the language is luxuriant and tender, creating cherished moments of togetherness away from 'the brazen world'. Here, a sense of inner peace, and the natural flow of time are still possible: in a room that overlooks 'elms/ Strung with sunlight' and in the conjugal bed 'stoked' with 'herbs in due season/ Tucked under wild sheets.'[23] In 'Aesthetic Knowledge', Alexander reminds us that 'We are creatures of this world' and that, as we paint the world and draw colors from it in order to paint ourselves, 'landscape becomes us'.[24] This poem seems to say that art is born from the world and it transforms us. Her work is strong and courageous, by turns confident and questioning, precise about the ways in which the experiences of life at times soothe and at times destroy us.

Yet, there are times when the suffering is overwhelming. Salvatore Quasimodo who won the Nobel Prize in 1959 'for his lyrical poetry, which with classical fire expresses the tragic experience of life in our own times' asks in his poem 'Upon the willows' ('Alle fronde dei salici')[25] how one can sing when faced with the howls of mothers who see their sons hung from lampposts; the invader's foot on the heart; and the dead abandoned in city squares. Oppression destroys people—even their laments. Poets, he answers, hang their lyres (*cetre*) on the willow, bereft of song. The lyre abandoned in public view is an image that represents the 'place beyond words'. The poet offers his silence, leaving the instrument to the wind as an expression of grief but also to show

---

[23] Meena Alexander, 'Darling coffee', in *Atmospheric Embroidery*, p. 5.

[24] Alexander, 'Aesthetic knowledge', in *Atmospheric Embroidery*, p. 3.

[25] Salvatore Quasimodo, *Giorno dopo giorno*, p. 41.

what violence and injustice obliterate. In this sense, the silence is not simply a sign of capitulation in the face of oppression; on the contrary, the image of the *cetre* hanging from the willow trees is there for the shaming, because the lyres recall the young men hanging from lampposts, representing, by association, their lives cut short.[26] The silent *cetre* 'voices' an admonition against barbarity with much more moral force than any preaching or any politician's war-time speech. Poetry, and art in general, can 'hold the mirror up to nature' (as Hamlet said of drama). The poem, to use Quasimodo's own words on the distinction between the poet and the politician, is concerned with 'the internal order of man' when confronted with the politician's 'ordering of men'. As such, the poem participates in the political moment profoundly, in its own indelible language.

An Incursion into the Mind of the Oppressor that Led to Writing a Novel-in-Verse

The above considerations of other poets lead me to my own questions about the characteristic features of language written in response to politics. In portraying a particular inner conflict, or in taking the vantage point of the observer, I drew on the experience of seeing people in oppressive conditions. I was also conscious of the public aspect of (published) writing. Somehow just sitting down to write about a memory did not seem so easy when so many other

[26] The image of the abandoned lyres is derived from Psalm 137, further establishing an exile-analogy: 'On the willows there/ we hung up our lyres'. See Herbert G. May and Bruce M. Metzger, eds, *The New Oxford Annotated Bible with the Apocrypha* (New York: Oxford University Press, 1962), p. 761 .

people were involved in the story. Should the language of my writing be morally impartial, or should it be fiercely passionate about issues, rallying the emotions of the reader for or against specific causes, for or against certain choices? Though the importance of the writer to the political system (both as conveyor of doctrinal ideas and as a figure of resistance) is a characteristic feature of communist societies, and is understood differently in the American society in which I live now, I still believe in the profound seriousness of the writing profession. In addition, as an outsider who needs categorically to justify herself in a new culture and a new language, I find that it is important to explain my values.

In this context, I would like to attend to writing that seeks to understand the mind of the oppressor. The oppressor, who to the oppressed seems virtually omnipresent and omnipotent, sometimes has the face of a friend who gains one's trust only to betray it, and at times has no face at all but is a string of words. How can one defeat or at least protect oneself from someone or something not properly understood, and how can the victim understand the mind and the language of the oppressor? During the past several years I have been working on a novel (now turning into a novel-in-verse) about a son who confronts his mother over her participation in secret police surveillance. She was forced to take him to an infectious hospital ward just weeks after his birth, to use him as a prop in order to spy on a woman who had been suspected of dissent. The book reckons with a generation which tries to put a shameful past behind it but cannot, because the past still remains a strong part of intimate family life. In the course of locating an appropriate form which could transform historical documents and personal experience into literature, deeper questions about what constitutes literary language surfaced, both as challenges and solutions to understanding the language we use when addressing historical trauma.

The story is based on my mother's own experience, when she was arrested while in the hospital with my newborn brother, the day my father demonstrated against Ceaușescu in 1983. In the novel, she figures as the target of surveillance. But the main speaker is Cecilia, the informer, because I have tried to understand what might have driven her into cooperation with a repressive regime. Cecilia's existence, and her predicament, are real, her work order appears in my mother's surveillance files: she was a mother who was actually forced to endanger her newborn child in order to entrap another new mother. Learning about her baby from my mother and from the files had shaken me: in 2013 my own daughter was only 2 years old and my son was 6. How could it be possible for a government to force someone to do this, and how could a mother carry through with the job without remaining damaged for life? I wanted to understand the mechanism of oppression as it was put in motion by language, by the narratives one learns to adopt in order to cooperate with the oppressor, and eventually become one. The portrayal of her character is based on researching her handwriting in my family's secret police surveillance file, my mother's story of the woman who befriended her during her hospital arrest, as well as my own experience of good, ordinary people who have made difficult choices.

I was keen to explore what happens to our minds, first, under the influence of the political orthodoxy of the time, and then under the duress of having understood that one had made the wrong moral choice. The plotline is completely invented. Here is Anton receiving his mother's letters after he has discovered her story in the declassified government files:

Anton felt disoriented by the secret-police speak of the informing letters. They were written in the third person, and she had referred to herself as "the source". She had built impersonal vignettes about someone's life that read more like play-acts in which the victim was trapped into confessing a political opinion with a seemingly innocent question. Her own feelings, her own opinions on the matter were sanitised. She herself was more or less a puppet whose strings you could easily see. There seemed no remorse behind the words, no sense of reflection. He had grown to hate her handwriting. Not long before receiving her letters he had piled the hundreds of pages inside large transparent white boxes and sealed them shut. Sometimes one has to let go of parents, he had told himself.

The arrival of her letters to him felt both like a lifeline and a fresh opening into a painful wound.

And here is Cecilia when she begins writing the letters to her son, after the initial confrontation:

The silence continued for months. Cecilia lived by imagining talking with someone, anyone who would listen to *her* side of the story in that fateful conversation with Anton. She had been walking around the block talking to herself, remembering Anton as a child, and as a young man. She lingered to notice how the buildings had fallen into decrepitude since he had left home, how she had aged, without realising, in the same way as those buildings whose eaves sank and gutters rusted, leaving brown streaks against the neglected cement walls. She was aware how different the story in her heart was from what had broken out in strident print, how easily she could be discounted now, even by her own son.

A memory of Anton crying or giggling keeps nagging her, the child's voice seems to fill the room with a sort of love, innocence. She tries to locate the memory but fails and goes back to thinking about conviction. Or desperation mixed with stupidity, disguised as conviction, she can no longer tell. It's a lifetime since, and the whole thing has remained like a deep scar from a burn: the yellow, brown and purple skin that looks disturbing to strangers is no longer noticeable to her because of familiarity. What is political conviction anyway? Is it, in all honesty, nothing more than being on the side of winners, rather than on the side of what is right, where most often people lose? A kind of safety in numbers? And what is morality? People do stuff to their children every day; think of those who abandon their families on the street and never return to them. Nobody bothers about those wretches. An overblown question, she thinks.

The most shocking aspect of my incursion into the mind of Cecilia—the mind of the oppressor—was that while I travelled along with her, imagining her intellectual and emotional life, I began changing my feelings towards her and her predicament. This should not have come as a surprise: her self-justification was nothing more than the very typical story I know all too well of how people became informers and were trapped into the job, against their will. I also had her recite the political orthodoxy of the time which became mixed with opportunism fuelled by hopelessness and material hardship, so common in the Cold War years. The more closely I examined how she made her choices, the more convincing her narrative became, and by the end of the novel my relationship with her character had changed. I began writing the novel in order to get rid of her disturbing presence in my memory (for years I hated her for betraying my mother, and reading the files exacerbated that feeling); when I finished writing I understood the complexity of the motives that erode our moral well-being. Her induction into the world of informers follows the classic recruitment methods outlined in the Securitate manuals: those who refused to follow the orders found themselves scarred for life.[27] As I finished the first draft of the book that eventually became the manuscript of *FOG*, I was both terrified and felt a sense of liberation. I felt as if I was answering for myself the question Mandelstam asked himself in his poem 'My time': 'My time, my brute, who will be able/ To look you in the eyes?'[28]

George Orwell opens his essay 'The Lion and the Unicorn: Socialism and the English Genius' with an observation about the language we use to justify participating in conflict. 'As I write', he says, 'highly civilized human beings are flying overhead trying to kill me', and explains:

> They do not feel any enmity against me as an individual, nor I against them. They are 'only doing their duty', as the saying goes. Most of them, I have no doubt, are kind-hearted law-abiding men who would never dream of committing murder in private life. On the other hand, if one of them succeeds in blowing me to pieces with a well-placed bomb, he will never sleep any the worse for it. He is serving his country, which has the power to absolve him from evil.[29]

We can do anything, including killing each other, if the motive from which we proceed feels solid. That solidity comes from a

[27] See the very well-known stories of Herta Muller, available at: https://www.theguardian.com/books/2009/oct/10/herta-muller-nobel-laureate-memoir and Oana Lungescu, available at: https://www.independent.co.uk/news/world/europe/romanias-revolution-the-day-i-read-my-secret-police-file-1838206.html. See also for context, Katherine Verdery's 'Romania's Securitate Archive and its Fictions: An Introduction', https://www.ucis.pitt.edu/nceeer/2013_826-01g_Verdery.pdf .

[28] Osip Mandelstam, 'My time', in *Selected Poems*, trans. James Greene (London: Penguin, 1991), p. 46 .

[29] George Orwell, 'The Lion and the Unicorn: Socialism and the English Genius', in *Why I Write* (London: Penguin Books, 2004), p. 11 .

narrative that is universally understood: it is noble to die for one's country, it is noble to kill for one's country, and it is noble to die and kill for freedom, or for the revolution. The complication, of course, occurs in the interpretation of patriotism, national pride, political and religious affiliation, and so on.

That interpretation is rooted in language. For the writer, this is fertile ground for thinking, as it has to do with the employment of language to effect a specific course of conduct. It is not poetic language, to be sure, but it is emotionally compelling language which affects how we live our lives. The literature dealing with this narrative of 'duty' can expose the language that leads people to sacrifice themselves and their own families for what could be a fatal misunderstanding of the 'greater good'. Such exposure might make us all better readers of political language and slow us down when it comes to embracing causes that damage everyone involved. Perhaps we should spend more time trying to understand how people lose their grip on decency and compassion, as much as we are repelled by their actions. It's almost too facile an exercise to study how victims overcome their condition, because we are attracted by the resistors, whom we invest with a sense of moral superiority, confirming thus our own beliefs. I think that a deeper understanding of the various narratives that contribute to oppression can help us protect ourselves against many forms of tyranny.

The following poems, about choosing words instead of weapons to fight injustice in a silent country, and testing the meaning of words against a constantly changing political environment, where language itself suffers, are of their own particular time. The poem 'In the Silent Country' is set in 1980s Romania, and 'Rings' is about

America in 2018. They bring to life two different times, each with its own complications, but reading them side by side gives me a 30-year perspective on language, on how it has changed in my lifetime.

In the silent country

When the hens climbed the tree to sleep and the dog was let loose in the
    yard,
When their children went to bed, she covered the windows
In the doors with towels and hung the yellow blanket over the curtain rod.
He went outside, around the farthest corner of the house, dug the
    typewriter
From its hole, then from the garage brought a stack of papers hidden
Behind tools in a box. They locked the room.

Both sat at the large oak table and put on gloves to hide fingerprints.
Each night, one by one, hundreds of pages darkened with communal
    demands:
Hot water, electricity, freedom of speech, freedom to worship, freedom to
    assemble.
Their arms smelled of fresh ink and the room was the sound of struck keys
Between two breaths. Not one star looked inside, but the wind joined the
    hush
Of shuffled paper. Before the rooster broke the news of dawn, he put the
    typewriter

In its white crate and buried it in the ground at the back of the house.
She stacked the leaflets in boxes with beans on top – same beans for
    months,
Wrinkled and dry like old thumbs. With the towels back in the closet
And the blanket down, the room returned to order, quiet and dark like
    the street.
They kissed the children in their sleep. Posing as farmers, they left for
    distant towns
Where he filled mailboxes while she watched for informers and police.

Hues of mornings changed with seasons, but the early sun
Spilled light over his face, over her hands holding the map.
At times, when they stopped to wash out the sleep with cold water, he
    could see
The dark of her eyes. Fists met at the market and in the store,
Churches were demolished, and no one said a word:
Those waiting in eternal lines, or those who saw the crosses kneel

In the rubble of saints and chalices. When they slept, words
Rose from the stacks and they breathed them as they were on paper:
Hot water, electricity, freedom of speech, freedom to worship, freedom to
    assemble.
They retraced in dreams each step: typewriter in the ground,
Papers behind the tools, gloves in the cupboard, the dark entryways
Where the words went, someone looking at them through a crack in the
    door.

Every night the words replaced them – *her pale skin, her long brown hair.*
They whispered into the sleep of others, in the silent country.[30]

The events evoked here took place between 1980 and 1983. To say that the situation was turbulent is an understatement: people were starving and dissent was met with such harsh punishment that those who opposed Ceauşescu's dictatorship were often thought to be insane or reckless, a characterization my father had to endure most of his life. The general silence functioned as an integument that protected people from persecution. Still, at that time when the general public hid itself in mute acceptance of tremendous hardship and when language was censored, some relied on the power of words in order to resist. I loved that faith and I inherited it.

---

[30] Carmen Bugan, 'In the silent country', in *Crossing the Carpathians* (Manchester: Carcanet, 2004), p. 11 .

My recent work takes on the colouring of the current situation in the US and transmits, perhaps, unease at how language has changed here since my arrival at the end of the 1980s. Here is a poem that takes all this into account:

Rings

The growth rings inside trees cannot lie,
They're like our bones which thicken with years
Of bending over children, grinding the wheat,
'Bone goes through bone',
Grandmother Floarea used to say.

Tree rings, each cradled in the next,
Each as evidence of what the world has offered
And how the tree has worked with it;
How one grew round the other,
Strengthening the core with its own essence.

And words? Do they grow like the tree rings
From our humanity? *Democracy*, from Socrates
(Who said it contains all of our vices)
To our lifetime when our virtues will not be elected
By our votes. Can we say delusion of freedom?

Grandmother said, 'I work so you will have
An easier life. I grind my bones for you'.
When you fell the tree, to see its growth rings,
You cut off its life. Cut off the freedom to see
How it is made, and you'll stand on a stump.

Plato told the parable of the boat steered
By its passengers: he said democracy doesn't work.
We each take a turn at capsizing our ship
In the still benevolent sea. There will be rings
In the water, where we go down.[31]

---

[31] Carmen Bugan, 'Rings', in *Lilies from America: New and Selected Poems* (Swindon: Shearsman Books, 2019), p. 115.

I write with the voice of the citizen, rather than that of the politician in opposition. There are writer politicians, who have taken that route out of concern, and for good reasons. But I am not one of them. The question that resurfaces as I write poetry nowadays is: how has my belief in language changed with my journey across countries and languages? Words travel with us, keeping us on an even keel, they function as a currency, or as a gift. In a work of literature each word brings a history of ideas and feelings with it. In my own experience of seeing words and stories taken out of one context and put into another, I have become weary at how they accrue and change meaning. The effort remains to return to the unity between words and experience.

There is also the simpler urge to describe the people in my life. Antoine de Saint-Exupéry was right to say that he tried to describe people in order not to forget them, because 'it's sad to forget a friend': 'Si j'essaie ici de le décrire, c'est afin de ne pas l'oublier. C'est triste d'oublier un ami.'[32] Memory, both personal and cultural, is a repository of our soul. The simple gesture of remembering a friend in a poem rescues cherished feelings from the flow of time, evidence that there is much goodness in the world too. The work of the writer has never been harder, and literature, the place where the big questions of the soul are debated and where hope can be sustained, has never had a heavier burden to carry. The language to which we all have a right, and use to explain our lives to ourselves, is given to us both as a gift and a responsibility. For me, the relationship with language is essential in establishing the sense that we can speak and write with the hope that we will be heard, for as Quasimodo has written, 'The true poet never uses

[32] Antoine de Saint-Exupéry, *Le Petit Prince* (Boston: Mariner Books, 1971), p. 12.

words in order to punish someone. His judgment belongs to a creative order; it is not formulated as a prophetic scripture.'[33]

Conclusion: 'Well, You'll Have to Change That': Carolyn Forché's Poetic Journey

I would like to end this chapter by having a look at Carolyn Forché's memoir *What You Have Heard Is True*, which is the story of her coming to consciousness as a poet and as a human rights activist.[34] Her book is also a confession of sorts: she speaks about the struggle between her inward-looking expectations of poetry and the public role she felt initially unprepared to adopt, and she speaks about that sense of being part of a story greater than her own. This story begins in 1977, when Forché was 27 and 'too young to have thought very much about the whole of my life, its shape and purpose. The only consistencies were menial labor and poetry and, more recently, translating and teaching.' She was already an accomplished poet, whose first collection had won the Yale Series of Younger Poets Competition, but looking back, she sees that in her early work 'there was no thread of purpose or commitment'.[35] Then a man called Leonel Gomez, from El Salvador, knocked at her door. In the back of his car were his two young daughters.

---

[33] Salvatore Quasimodo, Nobel Lecture, "The Poet and the Politician", NobelPrize.org. Nobel Media AB 2020, Mon. 4 May 2020, https://www.nobelprize.org/prizes/literature/1959/quasimodo/lecture/.

[34] A slightly different version of this discussion of Carolyn Forché's work has appeared in *Harvard Review* Online as a review of her memoir, *What You Have Heard is True* on 21 April 2020, https://www.harvardreview.org/book-review/what-you-have-heard-is-true/.

[35] Carolyn Forché, *What You Have Heard is True: A Memoir of Witness and Resistance* (New York: Penguin Press, 2019), p. 51.

Gomez's name was vaguely familiar to Forché: she remembered a friend of hers, the daughter of expatriated Central American poet Claribel Alegria, mentioning him the previous summer during conversations about political unrest in El Salvador. Nothing had prepared her for what followed. 'Are you going to write poetry about yourself for the rest of your life?'[36] Gomez challenged Forché, before inviting her to travel to his country with him and to write about what she saw there. She accepted his invitation, and over the past forty years has become one of the most outspoken poets on human rights, not just in Central America, but around the world.

Gomez wanted Forché to join him in El Salvador because he believed a war was coming on, and the United States had something to do with it. He never explained how he had come to be at her door, but in their first conversation he spoke of his conviction that poetry can convey across borders the suffering of others and their hope for a better life. Forché was initially doubtful:

> I don't think you understand, Leonel… Do you know how poets are viewed here? We're seen as bohemians, or romantics, or crazy. Among the poets I admire, there is one who waved good-bye before jumping from a bridge, another who put on a fur coat and gassed herself in the garage. Great American poets die broke in bad hotels. We have no credibility.[37]

Gomez simply countered, 'Well, you'll have to change that.' The war he predicted was extraordinarily bloody. Sparked by the inequality between the majority living in squalor and the wealthy elite that controlled the country, the civil conflict saw Marxist guerrilla resistance groups fighting against the US-backed con-

[36] Ibid., p. 49.
[37] Ibid., p. 53.

servative government. The government death squads terrorized the country, and more than 70,000 people died, many women and children among them. *What You Have Heard Is True* recounts the several visits Forché made to El Salvador between January 1978 and March 1980, and the extent to which those visits have marked her. She credits her experiences in El Salvador with moving her writing from the realm of the personal into the realm of the publicly-engaged. In the introduction to her poetry anthology *Against Forgetting*, compiled many years after her return from El Salvador, she defines 'poetry of witness' as 'evidence of what occurred'.[38] Such a poetry records extremity and brings together the public and the private in an uneasy but necessary dialogue.

Gomez asked Forché 'to learn what it is to be Salvadoran, to become that young woman over there who bore her first child at thirteen and who spends all of her days sorting tobacco leaves according to their size'.[39] With him, she went to the houses of those engaging in resistance and of those who were unable to resist. She risked her life in order to meet a radio broadcaster who reported on the death squads; she also met poets engaging in protest through their writing, a doctor working without proper medical equipment in an extremely remote area, and peasants sheltering guerrillas. Living among communities where people's spirits were crushed, she began to understand why the oppressed do not always fight back. After visiting a prison where people were kept in darkness, padlocked in cages the size of washing machines, with openings covered in chicken wire, Forché became sick, and Gomez said to her:

---

[38] Carolyn Forché, ed., *Against Forgetting* (New York: W.W. Norton, 1993), p. 30.
[39] Forché, *What You Have Heard is True*, p. 248.

You're exhausted, you're shocked, you're sick to your stomach, and you feel dirty. These things are what people feel every day here— and you expect them to get themselves organized? You expect them to fight back? Could you fight back at this moment?[40]

What You Have Heard Is True does not offer an analysis of the role of the United States in the country's civil war. Instead, we get glimpses of American involvement: Monsignor Romero, the archbishop of El Salvador, appealing to the United States to stop funding the Salvadoran army; the American war photographer who would become the poet's husband; the staff at the American embassy unwilling to leave the embassy compound. Leonel Gomez, her guide to this awakening, encouraged her to locate the sense of 'revolutionary' in her own work: 'You want to know what is revolutionary, Papu? To tell the truth. That is what you will do when you return to your country. That is all I am asking of you. From the beginning this has been *your* journey, *your* coming to consciousness.'[41]

Forché presents truth as something personal and individual, verified by the physical senses, and therefore impossible to ignore. The smell of burning human flesh, the look of exhaustion and fear on people's faces, the sound of gunfire in the walls of houses, the roughness of rugs used as mattresses: these truths cannot always be found in historical records, media narratives, or arguments about political partisanship. Yet, they are there, a part of objective reality.

In collections such as *Blue Hour, The Angel of History,* and *The Country Between Us,* as well as in her work as a teacher and a

---

[40] Ibid., p. 161.
[41] Ibid., pp. 331–2.

professor at Georgetown University, Forché has married writing and activism. One school of thought holds that only victims of history should tell their story, and that the duty of the privileged is to empower those who have suffered to speak out. This memoir suggests that those who truly take the time to walk in the shoes of others will themselves be changed, and when they speak out against suffering, they do so with authority. *What You Have Heard Is True* shows one poet's awakening to the suffering of others and to the power of words. I find it an important contribution to the conversation about the ways in which our private experience breathes life into the voice of the poets we become.

CONCLUSION

Lumina Mea

In the hallway of our house, next to our family pictures, there was a photo of Dad from when he was in his forties, wearing a white shirt. I remember wanting to talk to him, to explain to him just how disrupted and different our lives were, how unrecognizable they had become following his arrest. So I took the picture down and wrote a poem to him. The void of his absence was filled with a presence that I was able to create in words.

My sister and mother 'found' him in the poem, they read it silently to themselves, they cried, and this is how poetry opened that shared space of comfort in our grief. Writing mediated, facilitated this situation when my father 'could be' with us even though he was in chains, far away from us, not knowing when he would be able to see us again. Because my father was a political dissident, we were under secret police surveillance 24 hours a day and microphones recorded everything we said. Silence, though tormenting, was a way to hide our feelings, it protected us from interrogations. In writing I had both silence and words.

That first writing period in my life remains the most intuitive, direct, and spiritual. It was the time when the face of God appeared to me, its features like those of the saints in the Byzantine icons

Lumina Mea was published in MONK art and the soul/an imaginarium, on 16 June 2020, http://monk.gallery/from-america-new-essays/language-at-the-crossroads/.

Poetry and the Language of Oppression: Essays on Politics and Poetics. Carmen Bugan, Oxford University Press (2021). © Carmen Bugan. DOI: 10.1093/oso/9780198868323.003.0007

around the church: a gold halo around a face framed with white hair, eyes blue like Alpine lakes. God was benevolent and smiled at me. There was always a lit candle in his hand that I understood to be the candle of my life. Those years, when we lived by drawing just enough strength to make it to the end of the day, I knew our family couldn't possibly imagine the answers to our future and I relied on every image of God I could conjure to ease the pain. He appeared in the sky above the house, radiant like the sun, and next to the window at moments when the sound of keys clinking in the front door told us the secret police were letting themselves into the house. It was the time when I understood that the poems helped to heal the damage done to our family by those who had power over us. Those poems did not have political overtones, they were simple expressions of pain.

My grandparents taught us the thanksgiving prayers, those in which we asked for forgiveness, and those in which we asked for good health. There was a prayer for everything and for every day of the week, but my one constant request was for God to enlighten my mind—*lumineaza Doamne mintea mea*. I didn't understand then what a 'clear' or an 'enlightened' mind was, but I remember visualizing it as a clean, sunny room. This was my grandmother's kitchen with its large oak table on which there were always small dishes of salt and pepper, and left-over polenta covered in a white cloth on a wooden cutting board; the cupboard with the plates neatly stacked; buttermilk in a clay jug; the icons and the vase with flowers from our garden. Sun through the blue-framed window. And of course, the oil candle burning gently on the wall, beneath the icon of St. Mary holding Jesus.

Over time that room has become more spacious, yet everything remains orderly, simple, and harmonious. I still pray often for a clear mind. I learned from experience that one is often plagued by cluttered, disorderly thoughts that are hard to shake off. The need for simplicity and clarity in my poems, the rejection of obscurity and opacity originated in the childhood prayer where everything and everyone had its place. In almost all of my work there is an attempt to restore things to their places: parents to the family, memories to their country, language to its experience. Language is always at the crossroads as it follows us in our turmoil, our joys, the boredom, and the routine—so one cannot afford to take words for granted. Oftentimes I have been blessed with reasons to celebrate, but then there were times when I have doubted language too. At the times when there is need for *claritas*, more often than not, there is also the need for *caritas*, for holding the world dear in our hearts.

Many writers see their work as a form of prayer. Seamus Heaney, for example, in his Nobel Prize lecture, talks about bowing to his desk 'like some monk bowed over his *prie-dieu*' because, just like a monk, he felt 'constrained by his obedience to his rule to repeat the effort and the posture'.[1] Heaney's humility is very moving: unsure of whether his poetry could actually assuage and appease the conflicted country where he was born, he nevertheless placed himself in the role of those who pray for understanding and for kindness. His poem 'St. Kevin and the Blackbird'[2] based on the story of the saint, offers a vision of self-awareness, patience,

[1] Seamus Heaney, 'Crediting Poetry', Nobel Prize lecture, NobelPrize.org. Nobel Media AB 2020, Accessed 7 July 2020, https://www.nobelprize.org/prizes/literature/1995/heaney/lecture/.

[2] Seamus Heaney, 'St. Kevin and the Blackbird', in *Opened Ground: Selected Poems 1966–1996* (New York: Farrar, Straus and Giroux, 1998), p. 384.

and personal sacrifice in the service of life: the arms must remain extended so that whatever hope there is, can grow. Because the saint merges with the world around him, he becomes part of the 'network of eternal life'.

There is something deeply joyful and fulfilling about writing. It is animated by the desire to reach that natural and immediately recognizable communication that flows from 'heart to heart'. Over the past thirty years I have developed a series of metaphors to explain the process of composition: making bread, ironing, planting a field, giving birth, cleaning and healing wounds. When I think of writing as making bread, the water becomes our tears, yeast represents our feelings, the flour is that wonderful material of language that can be transformed with the temperature of our hands, the little bit of salt, the patience and the heat of the oven where the poem becomes an offering for the soul. Ironing is a powerful image too: if the table surface is not perfectly smooth, all the wrinkles show in the fabric of what we iron, so the metaphor serves as a reminder that it is good to know one's values before setting out to smooth the language into a perfectly crisp shirt that one wears in public. These metaphors come from the ordinary, domestic life, which, because of the circumstances of my family's political persecution in Romania, feels now like an extraordinary blessing.

Here is a poem I wrote while expecting the birth of my first child, where the holy oil functions to bring about the blessing I so much hoped for, and in the end received:

From the beginning

For Stefano

The river shimmers under the bridge;
Scales on the back of fish.

Broken ice in the pond glitters,
Life grows inside of me, prepares.

Now that I know you are
Moving and growing,
I make one cross with holy oil
On my belly and one on my chest

So we can breathe together
And borrow dreams from each other:
Me, your unborn imaginings about
World and sun waiting for you.

You, my blood in which I send you
Fresh food and words,
So when you join us here,
By the water, we can talk.[3]

At some point in her life, a woman may have two hearts in her body: her own and the heart of the baby growing inside. Her body transforms as it works to nourish and shield the new life. The waiting months are filled with anxiety, anticipation, and a new sense of responsibility. One feels a very deep sense of being grounded in the world, dependent on it, part of it. Then arrives the threshold of birth when the life which was hidden inside one body shows itself and announces its arrival with those first cries, when new lungs fill with the air of this Earth. The mother, forever changed by experience, returns to having only one heart. This is how we are all part of this world.

In recent years, writing poetry is a bit like this for me. Writing has become more playful and spontaneous. The transition between the state of inspiration and the finished poem has become more

[3] Carmen Bugan, 'From the beginning', in *The House of Straw* (Swindon: Shearsman Books, 2014), p. 61.

mysterious too. There is the urge to articulate something, then the senses are all awake, and the poem grows at the back of the mind while life in language follows its course. Images form and grow until one day they are born. When I am writing, the energies of the words bring me back to the intense solitude and yet, at the same time, I know that I belong to the world in the most natural and yet mysterious way. It's an awareness of being in awe at what the words can sound out. The language given to me had travelled through ages, had changed with stories, and had guided so many people. Because of this, the poems often take their own routes—not the ones I plan for them—and I am happy to relinquish control. Just like bearing children, writing poems is an experience where hope meets the marvellous. I will end this book with a poem that perhaps records the sense that in the vastness of language we can glimpse ourselves, one moment at the time:

Water ways

For Alisa, who shouted, 'Mommy, I keep losing your steps!'

The water is writing on sand
Many drafts of the same story,

One more shimmering than the next.
I go there to memorize their turns

And feel their calling power,
Wrestle with their yesses and whys,

I get involved, make footnotes on some pages;
The ocean erases them impatiently

Offering shells the size of my feet,
Shhh, it says, now listen.

CONCLUSION: *LUMINA MEA*

*

My daughter says the clouds try to bloom
Above the water—white hydrangeas—

But the water pulls them down;
Clouds are children of the water, I say,

It's hard to let go of children.
Under the bridge this morning the river

Passes for a mirror half fogged over—
Visions and revisions touch its surface

As we look on; mommy, my child says,
The clouds caress the water.

A white hawk appears above us
Held up by the warm breath of the earth,

The tips of its wings recall silver lining
Gliding out of view like a thought hard to hold.[4]

---

[4] Carmen Bugan, 'Water ways', *RC Alumni Journal*, 4, 2020, p. 1.

SELECT BIBLIOGRAPHY

Alexander, Meena. *Atmospheric Embroidery* (Evanston, IL: TriQuarterly Books, 2018).

Alighieri, Dante. *The Divine Comedy: Paradiso*, vol. 1, Text, trans. Charles S. Singleton (Princeton, NJ: Princeton University Press, 1975).

Aristotle, *On Poetry and Style*, trans. G.M.A. Grube (Indianapolis: Hackett, 1958).

Arnold, Matthew. 'Maurice de Guerin: A Definition of Poetry'. In *The Norton Anthology of English Literature*, Sixth Edition, edited by M.H. Abrams (New York: W.W.W. Norton, 1993).

Berlin, Isaiah. *The Sense of Reality: Studies in Ideas and Their History*, ed., Henry Hardy (New York: Farrar, Straus and Giroux, 1996).

Berlin, Isaiah. 'Two Concepts of Liberty' (Original dictation A). The Isaiah Berlin Virtual Library, Wolfson College, Oxford University, UK, http://berlin.wolf.ox.ac.uk/published_works/tcl/tcl-a.pdf [167].

Boym, Svetlana. *Another Freedom* (Chicago: University of Chicago Press, 2010).

Bromwich, David. *Moral Imagination: Essays* (Princeton: Princeton University Press, 2014).

Bugan, Carmen. *Crossing the Carpathians* (Manchester: Oxford Poets/Carcanet, 2004).

Bugan, Carmen. *Burying the Typewriter: Childhood Under the Eye of the Secret Police* (London: Picador, 2012).

Bugan, Carmen. *Seamus Heaney and East European Poetry in Translation: Poetics of Exile* (Oxford: Legenda/MHRA, 2013).

Bugan, Carmen. *The House of Straw* (Swindon: Shearsman, 2014).

Bugan, Carmen. *Releasing the Porcelain Birds* (Swindon: Shearsman, 2016).

Bugan, Carmen. *Lilies from America* (Swindon: Shearsman, 2019).

Conrad, Joseph. *Heart of Darkness and Other Tales*, edited with an Introduction and Notes by Cedric Watts (New York: Oxford University Press, 2008).

Da Vinci, Leonardo. *Notebooks*, selected by Irma A. Richter and ed., Thereza Wells (Oxford: Oxford University Press, 2008).

Deletant, Dennis. *Ceauşescu and the Securitate: Coercion and Dissent in Romania, 1965–89* (London: Hurst Publishers, 1995).

Djilas, Milovan. *Conversations with Stalin*, translated by Michael B. Petrovich, (New York: A Harvest Book, 1962).

Eliot, T.S. *Collected Poems 1909–1962* (New York: Harcourt Brace, 1963).

Eminescu, Mihai. *Poezii* (Bucuresti: Biblioteca Pentru Toti, 1960).

Forché, Carolyn, ed. *Against Forgetting* (New York: W.W. Norton, 1993).

Forché, Carolyn. *What You Have Heard Is True* (New York: Penguin Press, 2019).

Grossman, Vasily. *Everything Flows*, translated by Robert and Elizabeth Chandler, with Anna Aslanyan (London: Vintage Books, 2011).

Hill, Geoffrey. *Collected Critical Writings*, edited by Kenneth Haines (New York: Oxford University Press, 2008).

Josipovici, Gabriel. 'The Myth of the Native Language'. *Raritan*, XXXIX (1), Summer 2019.

Kaminskij, Konstantin and Albrecht Koschorke, eds. *Tyrants Writing Poetry* (Budapest, Hungary: Central European University Press, 2017).

Leopardi, Giacomo. *Canti: Giacomo Leopardi*, translated by Jonathan Galassi (New York: Farrar, Straus and Giroux, 2012).

London, Jack. *The Call of the Wild* (London: Puffin Books, 2015).

Manea, Norman. *The Fifth Impossibility: Essays on Exile and Language* (New Haven, CT, Yale University Press, 2012).

Mandelstam, Osip. *Selected Poems*, translated by James Greene (London: Penguin, 1991).

Matar, Hisham. *The Return: Fathers, Sons, and the Land in Between* (New York: Random House, 2016).

Mill, John Stuart. 'On Liberty'. In *The Norton Anthology of English Literature*, Sixth Edition, ed., M.H. Abrams (New York: W.W.W. Norton, 1993).

Milosz, Czeslaw. *The Witness of Poetry* (Cambridge, MA: Harvard University Press, 1983).

Milosz, Czeslaw. *New and Collected Poems 1931–2001* (New York: Allen Lane, 2001).

Milosz, Czeslaw. *To Begin Where I Am*, ed., Bogdana Carpenter, translated by Madeline G. Levine (New York: Farrar, Straus and Giroux, 2002).

Nabokov, Vladimir. *Speak, Memory* (New York: Everyman's Library, 1999).

Neruda, Pablo. *Memoirs*, translated by Hardie St. Martin (London: Souvenir Press, 2004).

Orwell, George. *Why I Write* (London: Penguin Books, 2004).

Preminger, Alex and T.V.F. Brogan, eds. *The New Princeton Encyclopedia of Poetry and Poetics* (Princeton, NJ: Princeton University Press, 1993).

Quasimodo, Salvatore. *Giorno dopo giorno*, con una introduzione di Carlo Bo (Milan: Mondadori, 1947).

Quasimodo, Salvatore. 'The Poet and the Politician'. Nobel Lecture, NobelPrize.org. Nobel Media AB 2020, Mon. 4 May 2020 https://www.nobelprize.org/prizes/literature/1959/quasimodo/lecture/.

Ricks, Christopher and Leonard Michaels. *The State of the Language* (Berkeley: University of California Press, 1990).

Roberts, J.M. *The Penguin History of the Twentieth Century* (London: Penguin, 1999).

Rousseau, Jean-Jacques. *The Social Contract*, translated by Maurice Cranston (London: Penguin Books, 1968).

Saint-Exupéry de, Antoine. *Wind, Sand, and Stars*, translated by Lewis Galantière (New York: Harcourt, 1967).

Shakespeare, William. *The Riverside Shakespeare*, edited by G. Blakemore Evans (Boston: Houghton Mifflin Company, 1974).

Soyinka, Wole. *Selected Poems: Idanre, A Shuttle in the Crypt, Mandela's Earth* (London: Methuen, 1989).

Steiner, George. *Language and Silence: Essays on Language, Literature and the Inhuman* (New York: Atheneum, 1972).

Surdukowski, Jay. 'Is Poetry a War Crime? Reckoning for Radovan Karadzic the Poet-Warrior'. *Michigan Journal of International Law* 26(2) (2005), 673–99.

Surdukowski, Jay. 'The Sword and the Shield: The Uses of Poetry at the War Crimes Trial of Radovan Karadžić, the Poet-Warrior'. *Law & Literature* 31(3) (2019), 333–55, DOI: 10.1080/1535685X.2018.1530907.

Szirtes, George. *New and Collected Poems* (Northumberland: Bloodaxe Books, 2008).

Szirtes, George. *The Photographer at Sixteen* (London: MacLehose Press, 2019).

Unamuno de, Miguel. *The Tragic Sense of Life*, translated by J.E. Crawford Flitch (New York: Dover Publications, 1954).

Virgil. *The Aeneid*, revised edition, translated by David West (London: Penguin, 2003).

Whitman, Walt. *Leaves of Grass* (New York: New American Library, 1955).

Wordsworth, William. 'Preface to *Lyrical Ballads*'. In *The Norton Anthology of English Literature*, Sixth Edition, ed., M.H. Abrams (New York: W.W.W. Norton, 1993).

INDEX

INDEX